W9-BHO-890

Collectors' Guide to
Antique American Silver

Collectors'
Guide to

Antique American
Silver

by Marvin D. Schwartz

BONANZA BOOKS · NEW YORK

Copyright © 1975 by Marvin D. Schwartz
All rights reserved.

This 1982 edition is published by Bonanza Books,
distributed by Crown Publishers, Inc.,
by arrangement with Doubleday & Company, Inc.

Manufactured in the United States of America

Library of Congress Cataloging in Publication Data

Schwartz, Marvin D.
        Collectors' guide to antique American silver.
        Reprint. Originally published: 1st ed. New
York: Doubleday, 1975.
        Bibliography: p.
        Includes index.
        1. Silverwork—United States—Collectors
and collecting.   I. Title.
NK7112.S38   1982   739.2′3773   82-1227
                                                                    AACR2

ISBN: 0-517-320924

    h   g   f   e   d   c   b   a

Contents

OTHER BOOKS BY MARVIN D. SCHWARTZ

Collectors' Guide to Antique American Clocks
Collectors' Guide to Antique American Glass
Collectors' Guide to Antique American Ceramics
New York Times Book of Antiques (with Betsy Wade)
History of American Porcelain (with Richard Wolf)

Illustrations

Introduction

Antique American silver has attracted collectors because its design is restrained and the quality of workmanship is consistently high. With only a few glaring exceptions, the statement is as true of later work as of that produced before 1830, suggesting that the same esthetic standard was followed late as early. Since a working definition of the word antique today is anything used decoratively that is not in current production, collectors have discovered that fine silver was made relatively recently as well as in colonial times. No matter what the fashion of a given period has dictated, American designers have tempered their work with appropriate restraint. When tracing the history of American silver designs it is possible to see how international fashions were adapted to American use and how, despite the variety of design between 1650 and 1940, there is a recognizable American approach.

Collecting silver is inspired at least partly by the fact that it is a precious metal. For some this means that their investment is safe; others find an element of romance in the fact that there is value in the raw material. They know that the best craftsmen of any era have applied their talents to shaping, engraving, or embossing precious metals. Silver had been second only to gold in value and reserved, along with gold, for fashioning particularly fine objects intended essentially for display. The craftsman who worked silver was equally capable of dealing with gold, and, in fact, he was called a goldsmith until late in the eighteenth century. Probably, he made more objects of gold than silver before the sixteenth-century influx of silver from South America. The sixteenth-century Spanish conquest had made a vast supply of silver available at the very moment that the market for luxuries was broadening. The merchants, the craftsmen, and the professionals—the group that might be considered middle class—had assumed more prominent roles in the community by the sixteenth century and they were able to afford luxuries such as fine ceramics and silver, if not gold. This middle-class group was to dominate the American communities where silversmiths' work was important as early as the seventeenth century.

The market for silver has grown continually from the seventeenth to the twentieth century as middle-class taste has spread, but there have been some esthetic problems. Design in the nineteenth century involved a series of style revivals and experimental efforts that have not appealed to collectors. Also the quality of workmanship is questionable at times because of the necessity for lowering standards to produce silver that was within everyone's reach.

Collectors have tended to concentrate on work done before the middle of the nineteenth century when handcraftsmanship was giving way to factory production. They consider colonial and early Federal efforts by American silversmiths as able, restrained interpretations of London fashion with an instant appeal since collectors of American silver prefer simplicity in design. The later work is often much more complex in design. The proportions of forms have to be studied to be enjoyed. Embellishments sometimes appear overwhelming since many nineteenth-century manufacturers were very ambitious in their desire to produce impressive work. The persistent and the earnest collector will discover that although nineteenth-century fashions often demanded more ornamentation than they believe necessary, the American makers succeeded in applying the restraint they preferred.

The second phase of the problem with collecting later material actually begins with late eighteenth-century work. As the demand for silver grew, a large part of that demand was for bargain pieces. Many aspiring to middle-class status were anxious to acquire the obvious luxuries such as silver as quickly as possible. They were willing to compromise on quality, and they settled for interpretations of fashionable designs made by short-cut methods. Instead of making a bowl out of a single sheet laboriously hammered into shape, pieces were quickly cut and seamed. These were generally made shoddily and they have little appeal to the collector who is interested in fine workmanship. On the other hand, some collectors find a charm in the awkward shapes made to appeal to popular taste. They regard the badly made silver as a kind of folk art.

Collectors interested in silver have a variety of challenges to face. They have to decide whether they want to concentrate on a style, on a particular form, or be more versatile and acquire whatever appeals. Considering cost brings up the question of investment since the cost of many pieces is high. A porringer of the eighteenth century by a maker of no particular renown will sell for about the price of a compact car. A coffeepot will be in the price range of a Rolls. After ten years of driving the compact car will be worthless. The Rolls has a high resale value and is sometimes worth more old than new. With antique silver, many collectors expect to be able to make a profit after several years of enjoying a piece. Antique silver prices have been rising steadily, but the situation is very much like that with the cars, and the expensive coffeepot will have increased in value more than many inexpensive objects. Records of auctions in the 1970s have revealed that many nice but relatively small and insignificant examples brought a bit less than they had in the 1960s. On the other hand, one Paul Revere tea set which had cost $35,000 in the 1960s was auctioned for $76,000 a few years later. Another example of the same maker had been sold for over a hundred thousand dollars. That is several times the amount it would have brought five years earlier. The single rule that may be formulated from the evidence of the antique silver market is that the rarest and most famous examples are the safest investment.

For the person not prepared to spend large sums, silver collecting can also be instructive, amusing, and even a good investment if the right field is selected. The silver that is inexpensive is the relatively ignored work of the late nineteenth century. The good investments are examples by the famous makers of that era. Tiffany and Gor-

ham are the latter-day Paul Reveres. Work by these two manufacturers is already in demand. Pieces by either bearing prices that are
within reason, but more expensive than most work of that period,
will probably increase in value more than that by unknowns.

Collecting is really not the best way to make money. Questions of
taste determine many of the fluctuations in price in the silver market
as much as economics, and neither is as predictable as it might be.
It is wiser to look upon collecting as a hobby that should not be
more costly than sailing or skiing.

Collectors would do well to consider the basic characteristics of
silver and to work out personal standards of what they consider
appealing. As a handsome shiny gray substance, silver has been used
in many different ways. The ideal American example of the eighteenth century comes in a handsome simple shape that shows signs
of handwork. The surface bears marks of the hammer used to shape
it and faint scars from the constant reheating required to keep it
malleable. The early nineteenth century offers small plain mugs that
are apt to be made of thin sheets that have been dented through
years of hard use. The contrast between fine work and the more
ordinary cheap products is equally evident in pieces on which roses
and leaves in high relief were the popular motifs in the middle of the
nineteenth century. There are lavishly embellished tea sets that
appear to be more elegant than the eighteenth-century examples
that must have served as inspiration. On the other hand, there are
mugs and bowls with the same motifs obviously made inexpensively
and having a different kind of appeal. Later in the nineteenth century
it is possible to find experimental designs based on the study of
Japanese and Near Eastern sources which are executed equally
lavishly or economically. By the beginning of the twentieth century
the traditionalist was trying to recapture the spirit of the best
eighteenth-century work, and the adventurous designer with more
subtle taste was anxious to rekindle the feeling of excitement that
was felt discovering an Early Christian silver cup in the corner of a
museum case.

Collectors will find that American silver is as varied as it is consistent. Whether the work of a single craftsman or the assembly

line of a factory, designs were handled knowingly with a modicum of restraint. At prices that range from a few dollars to thousands there are significant examples of antique American silver waiting to be rediscovered. Consider the possibilities suggested and choose a direction that will make collecting most enjoyable.

CHAPTER I

Silver-Making Techniques for the Connoisseur

Understanding how silver is made can help in solving the more challenging problems of connoisseurship. The fake or the wrongly restored piece can often be detected more quickly by the connoisseur who can discern inconsistencies in the way a piece is made. It is not just a question of how solder is applied or how relief decoration is hammered into a piece, however. The knowing connoisseur must become aware of the changing esthetic standards which influence the character of the technique. The seventeenth-century American craftsman was interested in larger-scaled moldings than his colleagues fifty years later, but each was equally intent on achieving a similar appearance for the finished product. Both believed the surface of a piece should show some marks of the hammering that shaped it. Neither objected to minor amounts of fire-scale remaining.

In the nineteenth century a shift in taste resulted in silver makers trying for completely smooth unblemished surfaces. The new esthetic made it easy to adjust to developments that changed the manner of forming holloware shapes. By the time bowls were stamped out by power presses, there was no longer an interest in textured surfaces that showed hammer marks.

As old silver is studied, the fact that technique is essentially a part of the expression or conception of a particular moment in time becomes increasingly clear. The methods of making seventeenth-century silver were suitable for that period but would not have been appropriate in the nineteenth century when there was a demand for complex ornament. Later work required the combination of machines and hands available to achieve the effect desired.

It is fascinating to see how details are transformed in the course of time. The leaf hammered into a seventeenth-century bowl differs from one that has been applied to a nineteenth-century example. The first appears to be a record of light and shadow while the later one is rendered in much greater detail. But it is not simply a matter of details that suggest differences in when pieces were made. Proportions also vary radically from era to era. Nonetheless, the starting point for the collector should be understanding the process of making silver objects.

The traditional techniques used by silversmiths working in small shops have not changed very radically through the centuries. Mass production, on the other hand, is responsible for a very large percentage of all the silver made since the middle of the nineteenth century, and today's esthetic philosophy takes into consideration the new techniques that make slicker work possible. We should begin by tracing the steps of an individual silversmith and then consider the changes introduced to mass-production silver.

It is important to remember that the craftsman who produced silver objects before the advent of mass production also worked in the more treasured gold, so that he was called a goldsmith. Gold had always been more revered, although silver was grouped with it as the second most precious metal. Through the ages silver and gold have always been rare and each is relatively easy to form because of its malleability. Gold has the added merit of permanence since it doesn't tarnish.

Gold and silver are also too soft to be used except in combination with another metal for strengthening. In the case of silver, the standard alloy consists of 925 parts silver to 75 parts copper. This is known as sterling silver. The gold alloy is measured in karats. A karat is 1/24 part pure gold, so that a 24-karat piece would be pure gold and too soft to use. Fourteen karats are frequently used today, but 18-karat gold was popular in the nineteenth century.

In England and many parts of the continent, the purity of the precious metals employed in making objects was tested by the guild or a government assay office, and pieces with the proper silver or gold content were marked appropriately. American silversmiths were rarely controlled by such testing, with the exception of Baltimore where an assay office operated from 1814 to 1830. Americans employed an honor system that was successful because results that have been assayed suggest that the silversmith had integrity. Many countries introduced special marks applied after a piece was tested to show its quality, but Americans rarely marked anything but their name on a piece.

Traditional silversmithing, the way of making silver particularly important before the nineteenth century, involves working the metal while it is hot. Activity in a small shop revolves around a source of heat—ordinarily charcoal, electric, or gas. In colonial times the apprentice would be sent to the local bakeshop to obtain charcoal which was a by-product of making bread.

Colonial American craftsmen had some problem procuring silver as a raw material, so it was often obtained by melting down old pieces or coins. Early account books have references to customers who supplied the craftsman with coins or old-fashioned wares that could be melted into ingots. Alternatively, ingots might be purchased by the craftsman. The silversmith can chose one of several ways to shape a holloware object. The ingot may be forged into shape by heavy hammering or it may be transformed into a sheet the required thickness of the final product and hammered less heavily and extensively. When the silversmith begins with an ingot the technique is called forging. When a proper-sized disc the thickness of the final product is used, the technique is known as raising. Either way, the hammering is done with the aid of anvils of various shapes. Forging and raising both involve using a single piece of metal for the basic shape.

At first glance it isn't easy to distinguish a forged piece from a raised piece. In fact, it isn't much easier to recognize the more radical departure in technique, seaming, which involves cutting forms from sheets of silver that are to be bent and soldered into shape. A good job of seaming is invisible on the surface, although solder marks show inside. Seaming is a simplified method of creating holloware that became popular late in the eighteenth century.

No matter what method is used to shape a piece, the metal must be reheated constantly during production by a process known as annealing. Annealing scars the surface as does the hammering for the raising, forging, or seaming which leaves uneven marks. Finishing a piece required the use of special planishing hammers to smooth the surface and a polishing to rub off the blackening of the fire.

There are a variety of ways of decorating silver. Ornament may be scratched or engraved into the surface if flat decoration is desired. Relief ornament can be introduced by employing one of a number of techniques. The simplest way to use relief is by applying cast ornament. Decoration is formed in a mold and the results are soldered on.

The surface may also be ornamented by a process known as *repoussé*. This involves hammering a design into a surface from the reverse side. Often, to reduce the risk of cracking, the piece being decorated is set in a tray of pitch to provide a backing capable of withstanding the blows applied to create the pattern. For bowls, special "snarling" tools have to be used to enable the craftsman to work from the inside. Punches or stamps are sometimes among the tools used to broaden the possibilities of the *repoussé* technique. Embossing is the name of another technique for applying relief ornament by punching on dies with decorative motifs. These dies are also applied from the inside. Besides the elaborate patterns, *repoussé* may be employed for simple fluting or narrow bands of gadrooning. Decorating from the outside is generally reserved for works in lower relief. When the dies or punches are hammered on from the outside of a piece, the method is called chasing. This is a process that changes the lines of the metal without removing any of it, which differentiates it from engraving—a cutting process that involves a certain loss of metal.

The techniques used by the small shops producing silver varied only subtly through the centuries until manufacturing was affected by technological innovation. The introduction of power machinery in the late eighteenth century first influenced the raw material. Silver rolled out mechanically in mills is thinner than the metal hammered by hand from ingots. The speed-up reduced prices, and one result was the amount of silver made increased tremendously after the Revolution. Inexpensive, quickly made work became common along with the more-to-be expected finely made pieces. The inexpensive shoddy work poses problems for connoisseurs since it is authentic, characteristic of its time, but not always very attractive.

The demand for cheap elegance that resulted in speeding up the process of making silver inspired the introduction of any number of new gadgets. Typical of these is the wheel for engraving which enabled the craftsman to apply a regular wavelike line with little effort.

In a New York newspaper, the *American Citizen and General Advertiser* (October 3, 1801), Thomas Bruff of Chestertown, Maryland, advertised a "machine for manufacturing silver spoons" capable of turning out 180 spoons an hour. The machine was patented and was one of many that were devised to simplify silver production. In Providence, Rhode Island, before 1800 there were several manufacturers mass-producing single objects such as spoons. or thimbles. Unfortunately, piecing together the development of large-scale silver production is difficult because though evidence of isolated activities has survived, we have only an incomplete story. For one thing, just how early the power machinery was used for silver is hard to say. It was exploited in the spinning techniques that were introduced in the production of hollowares. This was a method of turning the metal on lathes to shape it—the desired forms were pressed against the moving metal. While it isn't clear when the earliest spun silver was made, the technique was popular for Britannia and pewter early in the nineteenth century. Many early nineteenth-century silver shops must have been large enough for mass production, but the records do not prove that there was anything but increased activity. Silver was supposed to be the product of a highly skilled craftsman. Even when shops grew and a limited mass production was introduced, the image of silver as precious and the work of a specialist was retained. It was fine to know that Duncan Phyfe had a hundred men making furniture but not to realize that John W. Forbes, a silversmith working in New York at the same time, did not hammer out every detail of the silver he sold.

The shops in the larger cities adapted limited labor-saving devices, but introduced no radical innovations in production. Mechanical engraving, stamped bands of ornament soldered on, and cutout decoration of the simplest type were characteristic of ordinary efforts of the early nineteenth century.

On the other hand, the choicest efforts of the period were more elaborate and ambitious than eighteenth-century examples. Handsomely detailed figures cast in relief were applied to large urn forms that were inspired by famous ancient Roman prototypes. An 1835 inkstand by Obadiah Rich has dogs represented on its stand in castings that may have been designed by Horatio Greenough, an important sculptor of the time. There is no restraint in the richness of the decoration of the more important examples of the period.

The overall *repoussé* ornament that is encountered first in the 1830s was clearly the result of a new technique. The intricacy of the relief ornament, with the attendant refinement is in strong contrast to eighteenth-century work. It could not have been achieved by methods used a century earlier. To include the details suggesting the feeling of realism that nineteenth-century taste demanded, designs had to be applied with dies or mechanical aids. There is a similarity to the rococo revival decoration on furniture that was also applied mechanically. In both cases, the nineteenth-century craftsman or manufacturer was inclined to concentrate on the realism of the decorative motifs.

By the 1860s holloware forms were made on drop presses that are still familiar aspects of manufacturing. The forms were stamped out by presses that had great power. If not included in the master molds, decoration was applied by a combination of mechanical and hand methods. One method was to use dies to stamp out ornament that would be soldered on to forms. Also, engraving was often applied with the aid of machine power.

The number of machines used in manufacturing silver has not been tallied as yet because there are many different ways of combining hand and machine work. Suffice it to say, the methods of making silver since the early nineteenth century have inspired a new esthetic approach. About 1820 the change begins to be evident, so that Empire-style examples were the first to reflect a change in the attitude towards silver. In the seventeenth and eighteenth centuries the craftsman had been satisfied with subtle imperfections in surface. He attempted to simplify the motifs he employed. In everything he made the mark of his tools was never erased completely. From the early nineteenth century on, the polisher worked particularly hard to conceal hammer marks. By using cast ornament instead of *repoussé,* or applying relief decoration by hammering out dies, the finished product was slicker than anything made earlier.

The range in quality broadened in the nineteenth century when the market for fashionable objects expanded. Cheap, quickly made stylish work was included in the increasingly varied group of silver objects available. Between about 1850 and 1870 the greater part of the inexpensive silver produced was silver plate. Plating was applied to Britannia, nickel, or the so-called German silver by an electrolytic process perfected in the 1840s. The early plated wares were made inexpensively by manufacturers who were also making Britannia. They employed the latest mass-production methods to offer fashion at bargain rates. After 1870, when the price of silver dropped, most of the silver-plate manufacturers also used sterling. However, plated wares have been an important facet of the silver industry, with ambitious designs characteristic of the later efforts. Well-preserved plated wares may be confused with sterling, but more often than not, the plated piece will have lost some of its surface in the course of a few years. A black or gray spot that looks like tarnish but cannot be rubbed off is the telltale indication of plated silver.

One of the basic challenges for the connoisseur is distinguishing between old and new silver. It is important to know the difference between originals and reproductions. While the difference should be apparent in the design, investigating how a piece was made is a good way to confirm the date. Even when fakes are made by the traditional methods, the quality of the workmanship in matters of detail and the way a piece is finished are very revealing. Recently a fake salt that was on the market fooled a few people. The model followed was that used by Jacob Hurd (Illus. 27), but the faker, typical of his kind, was much shoddier than Hurd. The parts were soldered together messily and the subtle textures and the remnants of firescale that would be pleasing elements on an eighteenth-century piece were exaggerated. Hammer marks on the fake salt are more obvious and the surface is brighter. The texture of regular hammer marks on the fake is related to that of twentieth-century "arts and crafts" style pieces.

The connoisseur must consider technique in the context of a historical point of view to be able to interpret what he sees correctly. Besides knowing the basic developments that led to mass production, he has to be aware of the changing standard or esthetic. There are few differences in technique between seventeenth- and eighteenth-century silver, but the appearance is very different because there was a radical change in the scale of ornaments. The seventeenth-century craftsman wanted to create forms that were essentially architectural in make-up. Whether a piece was large or small, designs were monumental. In the eighteenth century, on the other hand, the attitude changed and forms were organic rather than architectural. Animal-form legs and floral detailing were just two of the myriad of motifs that made for the more intimate feeling of eighteenth-century work. Scale and the very character of the ornament changed again in the nineteenth century. Empire-style pieces had more glittering plain surfaces that were played up by the introduction of richly ornamental bands. Some of the decoration was cast, some was embossed, but either way ornament was ambitious. The objective was to achieve the monumentality that had been characteristic of design in ancient times.

Rococo revival ornament was even more flamboyant than the Empire work, but the scale was as small as that of the eighteenth century. The nineteenth-century esthetic demanded greater intricacy than was required earlier, and silver makers achieved it by using mechanical aids. Since dies were made to stamp decoration on pieces, the decoration could be more complex than it had been in the 1700s.

The modern technique of stamping out holloware on presses has eliminated the traditional textures of hammering. The most successful work has reflected this change in technique in forms shaped to look best with slick, shiny surfaces.

While techniques are often easily discerned by carefully examining a piece, there can be problems. Experienced silversmiths miss occasionally. The connoisseur should remember that technique is important because it can be helpful, but evaluating takes knowing more than technique to be sure of when and where a piece was made.

CHAPTER II

Seventeenth- and Early Eighteenth-Century Forms

The earliest American silver varied from the plain—almost functional —to elaborate classical designs. Although the era was one when Puritans dominated, the range of early designs shows that simplicity was not the sole criterion. On the one hand there are basic useful forms made of silver to add importance, and on the other there are decorative forms conceived with the richest ornament that must have been only for display. Some pieces are almost too functional to allow the connoisseur the opportunity to suggest when they were made, and others are typical of either the more restrained late Renaissance or full-blown baroque style fashionable in the seventeenth century. Whichever category a piece fits, its relationship to English work is obvious. American craftsmen were aware of English fashion and, more than that, felt themselves a part of English culture. In fact, the first craftsmen to work in New England were trained in London, and others who had learned their skills on the Continent were quick to adapt London-inspired designs into those that were distinctively American. Silversmiths who worked in New York where Dutch influence was strong, followed London fashion but introduced modifications to suit local taste.

The first notice of a silversmith that can be found in the American colonies is a Boston document. John Mansfield is recorded as a goldsmith there as early as 1634. Possibly the earliest piece of

American silver is a thinly made "strawberry" plate of about the same time. Discovered in England, the plate bears the initial M as a mark. Before his death, John M. Phillips, late curator of the Garvan Collection, was hoping to prove its attribution to Mansfield. The piece is closely related to an English group of early *repoussé* examples that have radically stylized ornament. They are late Renaissance but look almost primitive. Phillips called his discovery American because it differed from the rest in its details. The decoration appears to be more subdued than that on the others, which is regarded as one of the telltale signs of American craftsmanship.

More secure in their attribution are the objects that were made by the two Boston silversmiths, Robert Sanderson and John Hull. Both were prominent in Boston about 1650. Hull had been appointed mintmaster for the Commonwealth of Massachusetts when it established a mint in 1652, and he invited Sanderson to be his partner in the enterprise. The partnership produced silver as well as the famous Pine-tree shillings, and marked examples in the collections of a number of Boston churches are splendid datable documents of seventeenth-century activity.

One of the most fascinating examples of early Boston craftsmanship bears the mark of Robert Sanderson without that of Hull, since each also produced silver on his own. It is a two-handled bowl known as a caudle cup and resembles English work of the 1640s to 1660s (Illus. 1). A turkey is the main motif of the engraved and *repoussé* ornament around the bowl. This is surprising since classical cherubs or more simple acanthus leaves are more typical. While the turkey on this seventeenth-century bowl could be interpreted as proof of the menu at the first Thanksgiving, Sanderson was using the bird because it was then a popular Middle Eastern motif in exotic design. The same bird appears on early eighteenth-century furniture decorated with the imitation lacquer work known as Japanning. The exotic decoration did not affect Sanderson's basic form or handles. Both are classical and typical of the period.

The surface of the bowl is also typical in its subtle texture. The mid-seventeenth-century patron was appreciative of silver that retained some of the scars which occurred during the manufacturing

1. *Caudle cup. Robert Sanderson* (1608–93). *Courtesy, The Henry Francis du Pont Winterthur Museum.*

process. Burnishing and polishing could have gone farther, but the silversmith stopped to leave an uneven surface because his patrons evidently liked the texture of hammer marks and the very mild imperfections of the fire-scale when it was not entirely removed.

Cast handles in caryatid form are found on English, Dutch, and German examples besides the American. All are cast from similar molds. These handles were part of a repertory of design that was international, but in this context they are an element of a distinctively American design. The forms and the details selected by Sanderson might have been used on the Continent or in England, but his manner differed from those of Old World silversmiths. The decoration is flatter and a less dominant factor in the overall design on American examples.

Tankards were a popular form in American silver from the seventeenth century to the early nineteenth. Although details vary, the basic design was more or less constant. In the later examples, curving sides often replaced the straight ones of the tapering cylinders which were characteristic from the earliest days. The standard tankard form was very close to English models of the late seventeenth century. A covered drinking vessel of essentially functional design, there was a closer connection with the wooden versions seen in seventeenth-century Dutch paintings than Continental silver examples. The earliest Massachusetts examples are relatively plain and squat. Jeremiah Dummer, who was the first native-born silversmith to be identified, made a typical example in about 1676 (Illus. 2). The top is flat and stepped with an engraved border around the rim. The base has simple, bold moldings that are less delicate than those on examples made a century later. The thumbpiece, which is plain and conical, is unusual and cast examples in scroll patterns are more typical. The photograph shows the mark, I D over a fleur-de-lis in a heart-shaped punch, which is typical of the early work.

Edward Winslow, a Boston craftsman who learned silversmithing from Dummer used E W over a fleur-de-lis as his early mark and a plain E W later. Winslow lived in Boston from 1669 to 1753. The tankard illustrated (Illus. 3) dates from about 1690 to 1700 and represents a later step in the evolution of the form. The most notable difference from the Dummer is to be seen in the higher steps of the cover. In addition, the decoration of every part is more complex.

2. *Tankard. Jeremiah Dummer (1645–1718), about 1676. Courtesy, The Henry Francis du Pont Winterthur Museum.*

3. *Tankard. Edward Winslow (1669–1753). The Cleveland Museum of Art, gift of Hollis French.*

The dolphin-and-mask thumbpiece and the cherub at the bottom of the handle are both elements of end-of-the-century design, as are the more delicate base moldings and the relief pattern flanking the hinge. A comparison of the two tankards shows differences in proportion that can be attributed to the difference in time. Proportions lightened in the eighteenth century. A review of other Boston examples of the same period would include several with similar dolphin-and-mask thumbpieces. There are contemporary examples with variations in detail, but the proportions and the scale of the ornament are set in a given period.

Local taste determined design to some extent so that the craftsmen active on the New York scene were offering work that can be readily distinguished from that of the Boston shops.

The Dutch heritage of most New Yorkers was evident in their silver, but since the British flag flew over the colony, New Yorkers tended to combine English and Dutch elements in some designs. The typical early New York tankard is the perfect example of this selective combination (Illus. 4). In the Netherlands a tapering cylindrical form was not used for covered drinking vessels as it was in England, although New York craftsmen used it. As a tankard by Cornelius Kierstede (1675–1757) reveals, the basic English shape was modified for New York use. The base is embellished with a wire,

4. Tankard. Cornelius Kierstede (1675–1757). The Metropolitan Museum of Art, bequest of Edward L. Clarkson, 1929.

applied in a meander pattern, and a band of stamped leaves as well as the more usual molding which makes it thicker than Boston examples.

Cast ornament on the handle is found more frequently on the New York examples than those of New England, but it is not unexpected in Boston work. Early New York tankards are more likely to have handles simply soldered on the body without the more elaborate rattail ending against the cylinder. Proportions on New York forms are generally heavier and result in forms that are squat in contrast to New England examples.

Starting with the handle, an example by John Noyes of Boston can be related to work by his compatriots (Illus. 5). While the base molding, the thumbpiece, and the proportions are also fairly close to the other Boston examples, the gadrooning around the step on the cover is a good reminder of differences that occasionally occur. This gadrooned decoration was used on covers of English examples, which was the source of inspiration for Noyes.

New York silversmiths often were conservative in the 1720s so that John le Roux was not unusual at that time when he made a tankard in the squat proportions favored at the beginning of the century (Illus. 6). Nonetheless, Le Roux's awareness of the current fashion is demonstrated in many details. The moldings around the base and lip, for example, are as complex as any encountered in the period. The spiral turned thumbpiece and the sectional rattail on the handle are signs of later work and more advanced than the cast decoration on the previous examples.

As we develop an understanding of the esthetic that determined the appearance of early silver it becomes increasingly clear that American craftsmen were satisfied with results that might seem imperfect to an inspector on an assembly line today. Surfaces bruised by hammering, inconsistencies in details that might have been avoided but were left, are characteristic of the finest early work. Strangely enough the faker who attempts to suggest the seemingly casual approach of the first craftsmen, generally misses badly by exaggerating the scars and irregularities. Early hammer marks are never visible in the distinct patterns that are found on modern efforts.

5. Tankard. John Noyes (1674–1749), about 1696. Collections of Greenfield Village and the Henry Ford Museum, Dearborn, Michigan.

This subtle element of surface texture is evident in a very elegant pair of candlesticks made in New York by Cornelius Kierstede (Illus. 7). Kierstede's silver looks relatively thin and the hammer marks are particularly visible around the base. The basic columner form had not been given the classic treatment. A similar columnar stick of London manufacture made in the last quarter of the seventeenth

6. Tankard. John le Roux, 1723. The Metropolitan Museum of Art, gift of Giulia Morosini, 1932.

century would have been made of cast parts that are more precisely detailed. Kierstede combined the classical with Middle Eastern engraved ornament. The scenes were probably inspired by illustrations from a contemporary book of ornament. The linear style resembles that of pictures in the *Treatise on Japanning* published by John Stalker and George Parker in 1688, and for decoration there was

7. *Pair of candlesticks. Cornelius Kierstede (1675–1757). The Metropolitan Museum of Art, gift of Mrs. Clermont L. Barnwell, 1964.*

little differentiation between the Far and the Middle East. The capitals and the bases of the columns are made up of the elements more familiar on tankards and beakers. A border of meander wire has been used as an accent with a series of molded bands that have the same profile as those on much narrower beaker bases. Kierstede achieved his flamboyance by using what he had. The *repoussé* gadrooning with acanthus leaves at the corners confirms his abilities as a craftsman in a set that proves the existence of a distinctive esthetic. Skills are apparent in all the details, but Kierstede chose to create an almost primitive-looking representation of a fashionable form.

Much less apparently American is a small sugar box of 1702 by Edward Winslow (Illus. 8). This piece is one of the most elegant examples of baroque craftsmanship made in the American colonies. The vitality, inventive approach to classical motif, and its richness are basic characteristics that place it in the baroque style that flourished in the seventeenth century. The delicacy of the border around the lip of the cover and the bold swirl of the fluting around the body,

8. *Sugar box. Edward Winslow (1669–1753), 1702. Courtesy, The Henry Francis du Pont Winterthur Museum.*

the tight gadroons on one step of the cover as well as the lower part of the body and the acanthus leaves on both parts of the piece offer the sharp contrast so essential to exciting baroque design. St. George on the clasp is even more of a surprise to those conscious of the disdain Bostonians of the period had for saints. Although the design was London-inspired and the form close to London models, the ornament is just a bit more simple than that on English examples.

There are only nine American sugar boxes known. Four are by Winslow. One by Daniel Greenough of New Castle, New Hampshire, is much more modest in its ornamentation (Illus. 9). The coiled snake handle—a detail also found on English examples that John Coney of Boston used too—is the single elaborate element.

9. *Sugar box. Daniel Greenough (1685–1746), about 1715. The Metropolitan Museum of Art, Rogers Fund, 1946.*

Curving gadrooned bands and the punch work used as a border appear to be restrained in comparison with Winslow.

Gadrooning is a type of ornamentation that was one of the more popular devices to enrich simple classical forms. It provided an added luster because it increased the reflective surface of a piece. It is a motive that can be traced back to ancient classical sources. On the salver by Jacobus Van der Spiegel of New York, the relatively thin sheet has been decorated with two gadrooned borders (Illus. 10). The swirling reeds are wide and the overall proportions heavy so that the piece is characteristically New York. The same kind of salver by New England craftsmen would have lighter proportion and smaller reeds. (A salver by John Coney at the Museum of Fine Arts in Boston is typical of the New England type.)

Broad reeds on a more complex form by Edward Winslow suggest the change in taste that was beginning in the early eighteenth century (Illus. 11). The gadrooned borders make this chocolate pot reminiscent of classical urns, but the proportions are light since the form is elongated. The fact that the top has an opening and the handle is at right angles to the spout rather than on the same line shows it was used for chocolate rather than coffee or tea. The top

10. *Salver. Jacobus Van der Spiegel (1668–1708), probably before 1693. Courtesy, The Henry Francis du Pont Winterthur Museum.*

and the handle have cut and applied ornament that is typical of early eighteenth-century work.

A close look at the engraving of a family coat of arms shows the ambitious style of the period (Illus. 12). Scrolls and leaves overwhelm rather than embellish the central decoration, and the overall design is flamboyant. The coat of arms engraved on a John Coney teapot represents the seventeenth-century approach (Illus. 13). Embellishments are sparingly applied with the emphasis on line rather than more subtle shading. The design is made up of a pattern of scrolls and leaves.

Silversmiths could not ignore Oriental inspiration when dealing with objects to be used for serving tea. Chinese and Japanese porcelains were frequently models for eighteenth-century silver teapots, tea caddies, and sugar bowls.

A squat New York pot by Cornelius Kierstede is a case-in-point (Illus. 14). The basic shape is more characteristic of ceramics than metal, but the cover and handle would have been very difficult to

11. *Chocolate pot. Edward Winslow (1669–1753), about 1700. The Metropolitan Museum of Art, bequest of A. T. Clearwater, 1933.*

13. *Teapot: details of engraved arms. John Coney (1655?6–1722). The Metropolitan Museum of Art, bequest of A. T. Clearwater, 1933.*

12. *Chocolate pot: detail showing arms. Edward Winslow (1669–1753), about 1700. The Metropolitan Museum of Art, bequest of A. T. Clearwater, 1933.*

14. Teakettle. Cornelius Kierstede (1675–1757), 1710–20. The Metropolitan Museum of Art, bequest of James Stevenson Van Cortlandt, 1917.

make in porcelain. There is a meander-patterned wire border on the pot more familiar on silver beakers and tankards. The molded spout ending in a bird's head is familiar on porcelain, but the leaf ornament, both cast in relief and engraved, are typical silver decoration.

Peter Van Dyck, another New York craftsman, used a more delicate model for his teapot (Illus. 15). The body is a globular form that would have been easier to make on a potter's wheel than the silversmith's bench but the moldings around the base and the lip are the more typical on silver. But ornament applied on the cover is more restrained than usual in that it is so simple, although that occurs on a few other New York examples.

A communion cup by Peter Van Dyck is plain but rich (Illus. 16). Van Dyck lived from 1684 to 1751 so that his career bridged several styles. This is simple enough to be considered with early work, but the so-called rattail ornament on the handles is not seen before about

15. Teapot. Peter Van Dyck (1684–1750), about 1710. The Metropolitan Museum of Art, Rogers Fund, 1946.

16. *Communion cup. Peter Van Dyck (1684–1750). Courtesy of Se-tauket Presbyterian Church.*

1740. The restrained strap handles were made both early and late, and the shape of the body is not a clear index of the moment the piece was made, although it links it with the more functional efforts.

Dram cups or wine-tasting bowls were made early. Several can be dated to the 1670s. The typical form is small and simple with spiral-twist fluted or caryatid handles. Sometimes there is a tree pattern in panels around the bowl itself. The decoration appears crude because the scale is small and represents a moment when the delicacy was not an objective. The two examples illustrated were probably made decades apart (Illus. 17, 18). One is by Jesse Kip, active at the end of the seventeenth century, and the other by Henricus Boelen, who worked from 1718 to 1755.

Silver chafing dishes were made by American craftsmen before the end of the seventeenth century. Reviewing a few examples that range in date from the end of the seventeenth century to about 1740 reveals strong consistencies in design. The claw-and-ball foot was

17. Drinking bowl. Jesse Kip, 1699. Collections of Greenfield Village and the Henry Ford Museum, Dearborn, Michigan.

18. Bowl. Henricus Boelen (working 1718–55). Museum of the City of New York, gift of Henry Ryder.

used early as well as late. These dishes are evidence of the elegance of at least a few dining tables before 1740 (Illus. 19, 20, 21).

The first period for American silver lasted until about 1730. It reflected seventeenth-century style as well as the earlier eighteenth-century English tendencies. The silversmith produced simple functional forms as well as the more elaborate and elegant baroque designs, and despite the rigors of American life he was able to keep in

19. *Pair of chafing dishes. John Burt (1692/3–1745/6). Collection of Philip H. Hammerslough.*

20. *Chafing dish. John Coney (1655/6–1722). The Metropolitan Museum of Art, Rogers Fund, 1941.*

21. *Chafing dish. John Potwine (1698–1792), about 1730. Courtesy, The Henry Francis du Pont Winterthur Museum.*

fashion when he wanted. While his work proves he knew what was being made in London, he was able to work in a distinctive style that was more American than English.

CHAPTER III

Eighteenth-Century Design: The Rococo

There is a change in fashion that occurs by the 1730s which made silversmiths concentrate on more delicate details to create work on a more intimate scale. Even a porringer that at first glance would appear to resemble seventeenth-century examples can be recognized as an eighteenth-century product if one looks closely. The plain bowl of the seventeenth-century porringer was transformed into a more intricate form in the eighteenth century. The early model was made with almost flat sides and a very mildly domed bottom. The typical eighteenth-century example is curved at the sides and the bottom generally looks like a plate with a flat border around the edge surrounding a domed area. Generally there is the punched mark of a tool in the center of the bottom. The seventeenth-century handle was most often relatively plain, but in the eighteenth century the more popular handles were in a pierced design called a key-hole pattern. The design, was determined as much by tradition as the current taste, so determining whether a porringer was made in 1690 or 1740 can be difficult.

As in the first few decades of silversmiths' activity in the seventeenth century, the American craftsman of the eighteenth century was never completely consistent. While he tended to ignore the more obvious standard seventeenth-century decorative models, he would vary from the highest fashion of elaborate London work to simpler, more conservative designs that are not so readily dated. The American who desired conservative pieces settled for porringers or tankards most frequently. Occasionally, the loving cup—that two-handled, urn-shaped, footed form with a cover—was commissioned late in the seventeenth century. Most often the two familiar forms were for those who liked standard designs while London fashion was reflected in more adventuresome salvers, coffeepots, and the like. Still another group of eighteenth-century pieces were made to be functional. There are funnels, strainers, and mugs whose shapes are determined by utility rather than fashion. However utilitarian or decorative pieces are, the collector has the challenge of examining specific work to be sure of authenticity. The problem comes up because both outright fakes and reproductions have been made. Mistakes by experienced connoisseurs suggest the need for caution, but that should not deter the collector.

Questions come up with silver in each of the categories because American silver is valuable enough to make crime pay. A plain English tankard is worth much less than its mate with an American mark. Rarely are there English and American pieces that resemble each other to such a degree that it is impossible to sense an English piece with new marks or with the English date and purity marks removed. The design will tend to be more intricate on a London manufacture. If marks have been removed, careful checking of the surface will reveal the places that have been smoothened.

The elaborate but new piece that is passed off as eighteenth century rarely is well made. Nonetheless, there are finely wrought new pieces turning up. Generally, the elaborate fake looks old because it has been battered, so one should be suspicious of any signs of artificial wear. Scratches that are applied too regularly, cast parts that are crisply smooth because the wear is from the mold rather than the years of use, engraving that is too deep and too messily executed are all signs of trouble. Connecticut or Virginia silversmiths working in small towns sometimes produced relatively crude results, which are never as crude as modern efforts to duplicate them.

There is not as much fakery as the cautionary statements might suggest, but the situation can easily change, and, more important, an awareness of where the fakers go wrong sharpens the appreciation of what is wonderful about American silver.

The silversmith was the most skillful artisan active in the colonies. He was able to work in gold and silver but often he also knew about other kinds of metal. Frequently he was able to repair or make clocks. Besides having the ability to use precious metals, he was often capable of understanding financial matters since his was a business that required capital. Traditionally, the silversmith of the colonial era has been regarded as the forerunner of the banker. The extent to which that theory is valid is not easily determined, but prosperous colonists did trade their coins for silver objects and they paid well for the silversmiths' efforts.

The 1730s mark the beginning of distinctive eighteenth-century styles in colonial America. It was the period when an intimate scale of design was first introduced. The change can be detected in the paintings of John Smibert as well as the furniture of cabinetmakers using designs in what is called the Queen Anne style. This same approach is evident in silver for the period in which there was a broadening of the variety of forms along with the use of more intricate patterns. Life had become more elegant for people on both sides of the Atlantic by 1730 so that there was a growing demand for decorative pieces. At the same time, some purely functional pieces were made in silver to prove the owners could afford extravagance.

A quick survey of American silver would reveal a certain consistency in design for about the sixty years between 1730 and 1790. For each of the decades there was a tendency to exploit curving designs in varying degrees of flamboyance. While there is a temptation to call the simpler variations early and the elaborate ones late, the designs used over the years evidently varied for other reasons. While the simplest designs might have appealed most to early patrons, they were not used exclusively by the early patrons.

Early or late, plain or elaborate, the style that dominated the middle of the eighteenth century was the Rococo. It is characterized by a consistent lightness in the scale of rococo design. Characteristic early designs tend to have a minimum of relief ornament, but later examples have a maximum of leaves and ribbon as decoration.

22. *Porringer. Adrian Bancker (1703–72), 1725–50. The Metropolitan Museum of Art, bequest of A. T. Clearwater, 1933.*

23. *Porringer. Benjamin Burt (1729–1803), 1750–75. The Metropolitan Museum of Art, bequest of A. T. Clearwater, 1933.*

The porringer by Adrian Bancker (1703–72) was very likely made after 1730, but it typifies the earlier type (Illus. 22). The plain handle design is close in spirit to seventeenth-century examples but the bottom appears to be later. The center area resembles those of eighteenth-century origin. The curving sides and the angled lip are close to later designs. The more elaborate, later handle accompanied by a more intricately detailed bowl confirms the later date of a porringer by Benjamin Burt (Illus. 23). This might have been made

24. *Spout cup with cover. John Edwards (1671–1746). Courtesy, The Henry Francis du Pont Winterthur Museum.*

25. Pap boat. Cary Dunn. The Cleveland Museum of Art, gift of Hollis French.

any time between about 1750 and 1775. The overall shape and more specifically the plate-shaped bottom are signs of the vintage.

Designed for feeding invalids or children, the spout cup is a form known as early as the seventeenth century. Eighteenth-century examples are bulbous forms with domed covers. John Edwards, who had made some jug-shaped cups before 1720, followed the fashions in adapting a shape used for mugs and pitchers in the 1730s and 1740s (Illus. 24).

The pap boat is a utensil for serving invalids a kind of cereal known as pap. Small and a little like a sauceboat, it is simple and evidently practical. The example (Illus. 25) by Cary Dunn gives one a good idea of the forms that could be made in the period. Essentially functional, the curving spout and the lip are classical elements which suggest the piece was made in the 1730s.

Buckles are an unusual form for colonial American silver, but they must have been popular in the eighteenth century. Early records include frequent mention of them and while few early examples have turned up, buckles such as one discovered in Plymouth, Massachusetts, during the 1960s are ordinary enough to suggest the form was common by about 1750 (Illus. 26). The illustration shows both sides and the flatness of the relief decoration would make it plausible that such buckles were not of extraordinary high quality when they were new. Buckles, buttons, and a range of small pins and boxes made by American silversmiths throughout the eighteenth century turn up from time to time. They are as often unmarked as marked.

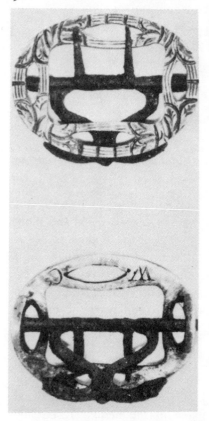

26. Knee buckles. Unidentified maker. Photo courtesy of Charles Strickland.

The 1730s, or possibly a little earlier, marked the beginning of using silver to make the more varied forms that were in demand for the table. The elegant services which had been reserved for the European courts were being adapted by the middle classes and salts, for one, became increasingly popular. The standing salt had been significant as one of the grander forms of the seventeenth century, but later the trencher salt, which was reduced in scale to be used near the trencher rather than in the center of the table, was the more familiar form. A comparison with any selection of English examples would reveal how close American and English models could be. American versions tended to be more simple, with the decoration less prominent so that the overall design would appear more functional. The low trencher salt is one form that Americans favored.

27. Trencher salt. Jacob Hurd (1702–58), about 1730. The Metropolitan Museum of Art, Rogers Fund, 1943.

Examples by Jacob Hurd and others have been discovered. Typically, the salts are octagonal with solid molded sides enclosing and supporting relatively deep elliptical bowls (Illus. 27). One example by Jacob Hurd (1702–58) of Boston follows a design that was used in London in the 1730s. The curving sides articulated by subtly curving moldings at the base and the lip represent the more restrained aspect of eighteenth-century design. In London the form was known as early as about 1715 and it was out of fashion by about 1740 when small bowls on curving feet became the characteristic form for salts.

One of the most elegant American salts was made by Charles le Roux of New York (Illus. 28). It has dolphin feet topped by female heads and joined by a rich garland. These salts were very likely made for John and Anne Schuyler of New York who married in 1737. They or the silversmith must have known a spectacular "State Salt Cellar" made in London in 1730–71 by A. Courtauld. The feet and

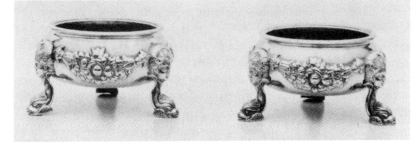

28. Pair of salts. Charles le Roux (1689–1745). The Metropolitan Museum of Art, Dodge Fund, 1935.

the female heads would seem to have been borrowed from the London salts which are ten inches high and must have been well known when they were new. Le Roux or the Schuylers could have seen the London salt, or heard of it, and decided to use its motives. If not, the symbol of the dolphin has an obvious connection with salt that comes from the sea.

Charles le Roux was one of New York's best-known silversmiths between about 1720 and his death in 1745. He made many of the small gold boxes given to men when they became "Freemen." The salts are evidence of his ability as a craftsman aware of the latest decorative fashions. Careful examination suggests that he tempered details to produce an article more subdued than the more daring London model.

In the eighteenth century, pepper, mustard, and sugar were more frequently shaken or cast out of a container onto food than salt. The cylindrical or octagonal tube-shaped container topped by a pierced domed cover, which looks like a salt shaker, is called a caster, pepper pot, or spice dredger and was used for anything but salt. The caster form was made in several sizes. One group with handles have been distinguished as pepper boxes. Actually the early records are confusing because one finds casters, spice dredgers, and pepper boxes listed. Gregor Norman-Wilcox, the late silver connoisseur, attempted to define the three according to size. In a book on English silver, G. Bernard Hughes said that the spice dredger was superseded during the 1760s by the handleless caster. To add to the confusion, Rufus Greene, a Massachusetts silversmith of the eighteenth century, listed a caster in his inventory but the piece, now in the Museum of Fine Arts in Boston, has a handle and is listed by the renowned Kathryn Buhler in her catalogue of the collection as a pepper box. The names of eighteenth-century objects are not always constant and the definitions of terms may vary at any given moment.

The simple cylindrical form is generally regarded as earlier than the octagonal or baluster shapes. A plain cylinder in the Winterthur Museum, which bears the mark of William Heurtin of New York, has been dated about 1731 (Illus. 29). It has a handle that is an undecorated ear-shaped band, while similar pieces occasionally have the so-called rattail ornament applied. The Heurtin piece also has an

29. Caster. William Heurtin, about 1731. Courtesy, The Henry Francis du Pont Winterthur Museum.

unusual base with a wider bottom band than is usual. The moldings at the lips of cylindrical pepper pots are often more complex, and consist of more bands than are found on the Heurtin example.

Octagonal examples most often taper toward the top as does the example by Jonathan Otis which may have been made about 1750 (Illus. 30). Otis worked in both Newport, Rhode Island, and Middletown, Connecticut. He left Newport during the Revolution and

30. Caster. Jonathan Otis (1723–91), 1750–75. The Metropolitan Museum of Art, bequest of A. T. Clearwater, 1933.

spent the rest of his life in Connecticut. Not much of his work has survived, but he made silver for churches in both Rhode Island and Connecticut that attest to his skills while suggesting that he might have avoided elaborate designs. Otis' work, like that of other Newport silversmiths, was essentially conservative and restrained. The caster resembles several other Newport pieces in the simplicity of the moldings and the fact that there is no handle.

Baluster-shaped casters are often relatively tall but they do vary in height as well as design. Early records often list sets of three casters, but they were also purchased singly. A caster by Simeon Soumaine that probably dates from the 1730s has its steep-domed cover fastened to the body by cast lugs of a type that are frequently called "bayonet" fasteners. The cover has a globular finial and the pierced holes are a pattern of circles and ellipses high-lighted by engraved lines (Illus. 31). Soumaine worked in New York from about 1715 to his death in

31. Caster. Simeon Soumaine (c. 1685–1750). Collection of Philip H. Hammerslough.

about 1750. A Huguenot, he had come from London as a child and managed to become one of New York's finest craftsmen. His efforts are among the most subtle of the early rococo, but he also made tankards and bowls typical of traditional New York output.

Casters with screw-on tops and bodies that have more emphatic transitions from base to neck appear to be later in date. Shapes vary but examples with hemispherical bases on molded feet that are nearly flat at the juncture and with straight necks are standard for the mid-eighteenth century. An example by Jacob Hurd has its pierced circular openings in a pattern of panels of latticework. It is topped by a squat finial (Illus. 32). Not very dissimilar is a caster by John Coburn which has a pine cone finial and holes that are framed by engraved panels that alternate leaf designs with the latticework (Illus. 33c). It was made for Thomas Wells along with the milk and teapots in the same photograph.

Urn or baluster-shaped casters are found mainly in the pre-Revolutionary styles, but once in a while the moldings or the tops are par-

32. *Caster. Jacob Hurd (1702–58), 1740–50. The Metropolitan Museum of Art, bequest of A. T. Clearwater, 1933.*

33. *Cream pot* (*a*), *teapot* (*b*), *and caster* (*c*). *John Coburn* (*1725–1803*). *Collection of Philip H. Hammerslough.*

ticularly delicate to reveal a later date of manufacture. A band of relatively narrow strings of molding on a caster are apt to be a sign of post-Revolutionary origin. When the urn has no neck, or when the cover is a shallow rather than a steep dome, a late date is also suggested.

Following the evolution of eighteenth-century design through the silver made in America can be difficult. Fashion was not always the criterion for design since conservatism often influenced taste. Americans, for example, liked porringers and tankards long after they had become rare in the London shops. More confusing was the fact that something as unusual as a typically New York paneled bowl was made as late as 1730 (Illus. 34). The caryatid handles and the *repoussé* tulips in the panels are both elements more easily associated with seventeenth-century pieces. The overall shapes are eighteenth century, however, and most of those known are of the 1720s and later. The bowl illustrated, by Jacob Ten Eyck of Albany, has the crisp decoration that is characteristic of the best examples. The design is related to Dutch work but not a precise copy of any specific model.

American craftsmen were more often content to produce forms closer to English prototypes than the bowls just discussed. London silver was sold in the major colonial centers and an awareness of the

34. Paneled bowl. Jacob Ten Eyck (1705–93), about 1730. Courtesy, The Henry Francis du Pont Winterthur Museum.

latest design was often evident in local work. Samuel Alford advertised in the *Pennsylvania Gazette,* May 24, 1759, that he could make silver following "the newest Fashions from England."

A salver by Simeon Soumaine of New York has a scalloped border and curving feet cast in patterns that reflect the rococo style in fashion in England and on the Continent (Illus. 35). The salver had been introduced in England in the seventeenth century when it was defined as a piece used for serving beverages since, by offering the drink on the salver, one avoided possible spilling. Much simpler versions were also made. An example by Philip Syng, Jr., of about 1740 is simply circular (Illus. 36). It is not very different from the footed salvers that were made by Americans as early as the beginning of the eighteenth century.

Casting was also the technique used to make candlesticks. The succession of eighteenth-century candlesticks range from relatively restrained classical vase shapes to elaborate rococo designs. Inspiration was from London with the models modified to suit American taste. Conceivably, English brass models might have served as prototypes since the designs were never as ornate as the English silver examples. A pair of candlesticks by Nathaniel Morse have been dated about 1720 and represent the simpler taste of the early eighteenth century

35. Salver. Simeon Soumaine (c. 1685–1750). The Metropolitan Museum of Art, Dodge Fund, 1935.

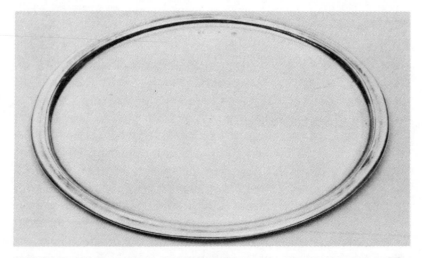

36. Salver. Philip Syng, Jr. (1703–89), about 1740. Courtesy, The Henry Francis du Pont Winterthur Museum.

(Illus. 37). The joint between the top of the baluster and the socket has an unusually large disc at the juncture that could not have been copied from a brass version. In fact, this detail is reminiscent of examples that were hammered out with ornate details. American candlesticks are very rare, and those that have turned up are of fine quality.

37. *Pair of octagonal candlesticks. Nathaniel Morse (1685–1748), about 1720. Courtesy, The Henry Francis du Pont Winterthur Museum.*

The casters and pepper boxes seem to have been replaced by cruet sets in the 1770s or so. The earliest examples are elaborate rococo designs that combine silver fittings with handsomely cut glass. A set made for the Ringgold family of New Jersey has bottles with their silver fittings from London set in a stand by the Philadelphia craftsman John David (Illus. 38). Probably made about 1765, the stand is a fine expression of American rococo ornament. The ribbon around the plaque for initials and the shell feet are restrained but elegant. The curving elements that support the frame that contains the bottles and the gadrooning on the frame are conceived with an economy of line that was common to designs in both London and the colonies.

Sauceboats are another form for the table that became more popular in the eighteenth century. Introduced in London during the first half of the eighteenth century, the earliest American examples date from the 1740s. The form was squat, the body elliptical, and generally on three feet. Many are plain and have their upper lips cut in patterns of scalloping. Others have more elaborate gadrooned lips. Handles are frequently ear-shaped, enough like those of canns to have been made from the same molds. Jacob Hurd's sauceboat was very likely made about 1750. It is the simpler type, with hoof feet, a cut-

38. Cruet stand. John David (1736–98), about 1765. Courtesy, The Henry Francis du Pont Winterthur Museum.

out lip and a small unidentified coat of arms in a ribbon-and-scroll frame (Illus. 39). Joseph Richardson, Sr., the elder of two important Philadelphia silversmiths, made a pair of sauceboats that are not much more elaborate than Hurd's (Illus. 40). The Richardsons produced some of the most ornate silver made in eighteenth-century Philadelphia, so it is something of a surprise to find sauceboats by the elder that have elegance without much decoration. The handles flair a bit extra and the feet are more cocoons than hooves, but simplicity characterizes the overall effect.

In complete contrast are a pair by Simeon Soumaine (Illus. 41). The handle curves less but the lip is gadrooned, the supports have shells at both ends, and a rich floral garland has been punched all around the elliptical body. Basically, the flowers echo the interest in the rococo style, but the bow of the ribbon that ties the garland just under the spout is as delicate as any neo-classical bow so that the inspiration may have been classical although the results are clearly rococo.

A soup tureen by Peter Getz of Lancaster, Pennsylvania, also seems to reflect the awareness of the later neo-classicism in a design that is essentially rococo (Illus. 42). Getz made this piece for Aaron Levy, a

Lancaster merchant, at about the time of the Revolution. Neo-classicism was the more adventuresome style of that moment, although the rococo had retained its popularity in America. Getz applied engraving with the scrolls, ribbons, and leaf ornament typical of the rococo. However, the decoration was used more sparingly than was characteristic of the more elaborate examples. The cartouche for the initial is even more linear, flat, and neo-classical. Getz's tureen is very unusual, since most American craftsmen did not make such pieces.

The tea table was a more popular place for silver than the dinner table in eighteenth-century American homes. Since tea was served to guests as a gesture of hospitality, the objects for it tended to be special. Tea services are very rare before the Revolution. Even in England they were not common before the accession of George III in 1760. Teapots, cream jugs, and sugar bowls were sometimes ordered at once, but often the pieces seem to be unrelated in design.

Cream jugs, also called milk jugs or cream pots, are generally relatively small pyriform pitchers on a base that might be solid or a tripod. One cream pot by Samuel Casey of Rhode Island is typical

39. *Sauceboat. Jacob Hurd* (1702–58). *Courtesy, The Henry Francis du Pont Winterthur Museum.*

40. Pair of sauceboats. Joseph Richardson, Sr. (1711–84), 1750–75. The Metropolitan Museum of Art, bequest of Charles Allen Munn, 1924.

41. Pair of sauceboats. Simeon Soumaine. Collection of Philip H. Hammerslough.

of many made between about 1750 and 1780. The lip is cut in a pattern similar to those found on sauceboats and the handle is a delicate scaled-down version of those found on the larger containers. Casey used a modified shell motif as the foot of the curving legs (Illus. 43). John Coburn of Boston employed a scroll design for feet on a similar example (Illus. 33a). The upper part of the handle is occasionally

42. Soup tureen. Peter Getz (working 1783). Collection of Philip H. Hammerslough.

rendered as a bird's head to add a note of whimsey to plain, essentially functional pitchers of this type.

A New York silversmith who has attracted many collectors, Myer Myers, was responsible for some of the most outstanding work just before and after the Revolution. The son of the caretaker of New York's synagogue, Myers was one of the few Jews to make his mark as a colonial craftsman. One of his cream or milk pots has unusually elegant decoration (Illus. 44). Flowers, leaves, ribbons, and even an occasional pomegranate are part of the *repoussé* ornament applied in curving panels which are characteristic of the more flamboyant rococo efforts. The solid foot has a border of gadrooning and the lip has a related rope band around it. The handle was cast in a graceful scroll design. Myers' simpler version of the same basic design has no *repoussé* ornament and a plain base but the handle and the lip are elaborate (Illus. 45a).

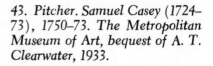

43. Pitcher. Samuel Casey (1724–73), 1750–73. The Metropolitan Museum of Art, bequest of A. T. Clearwater, 1933.

44. Creamer. Myer Myers (1723–95). Ginsburg & Levy, Inc., New York.

About the middle of the eighteenth century, Americans preferred the globular teapots that English collectors call bullet teapots to distinguish them from the more varied shapes that appeared earlier. The form had been introduced in London by the 1720s. It was generally made with minimal decoration, although engraving around the cover is not unusual. The pot by Jacob Hurd for M. Perit was probably made about 1750 (Illus. 46). The spout is plain but the finial is rendered as a pine cone. The foot consists of the kind of bold molding that was particularly popular in the middle of the century. John Coburn used the same basic shape for the teapot Thomas Wells obtained from him (Illus. 33b). The engraving is more elaborate and emphatically rococo in its ribbon-and-scroll pattern with the coat of arms framed flamboyantly. Cast ornament on the spout and the upper end of the handle are elements expected in work of the 1770s. The domed cover and the flame finial also suggest a later date for the Coburn effort than that by Hurd. The globular form was replaced by a more complex variation that is an inverted pear shape. The most impressive examples have *repoussé* ornament or applied cast decoration in rococo motifs.

The squat pear-shaped body was introduced about 1720. New York silversmiths continued to use it until about 1760. A mid-century example by Daniel Christian Fueter can be dated later because its finial is more elaborate than those made earlier (Illus. 47).

Traditionally, containers for hot beverages in designs with a vertical emphasis are called coffeepots. A few documents and very early Eng-

45. *Milk pot (a), coffeepot (b), and sugar bowl (c). Myer Myers (1723–95), about 1765. Courtesy, The Henry Francis du Pont Winterthur Museum.*

46. Teapot. Jacob Hurd (1702–58), about 1750. Courtesy, The Henry Francis du Pont Winterthur Museum.

lish example with an inscription inspire some questioning of how these pots were used, but for now the differentiation is practical. Plain tapering cylinder forms were used between the 1720s and 1740s, but shortly after 1750 an elongated pyriform shape, sometimes called double-bellied was just about standard for coffeepots. Myer Myers' coffeepot was rich in cast ornament on the cover, spout and

47. Teapot. Daniel Christian Fueter (1720–85), about 1760. Courtesy, The Henry Francis du Pont Winterthur Museum.

handle (Illus. 45b). John David used about the same shape but the gadrooning is more obvious on the cover and base, and the pineapple finial suggests that this would be an example of the rococo in its final stage of popularity (Illus. 48). Both reflect the very capable hands of talented craftsmen.

48. *Coffeepot. John David* (1736–98). *Collection of Philip H. Hammerslough.*

Sugar bowls are another form encountered when tea became the beverage served for entertaining guests. The forms of early examples

49. Sugar Bowl. Charles Oliver Bruff (working in New York 1763–83). The Museum of the City of New York, gift of Nicholas G. Rutgers, Jr., Mrs. George Coe, Mrs. Marshall J. Dodge, Jr.

were based on Oriental covered bowls. Porcelainlike delicacy was sometimes achieved, but more often the design was adapted to silver by introducing traditional silver moldings as borders. Myer Myers' simple sugar bowl is more pyriform than most porcelain, and the top is also more complex (Illus. 45c). On the other hand, Charles Oliver Bruff, a New Yorker active between about 1760 and 1780, kept closer to the porcelain model even though he applied two bands of rococo engraving (Illus. 49). Both Myers and Bruff topped their covers with handles that could serve as feet when the cover was turned over and placed on a table.

In complete contrast to the simplicity of the other two examples is a bowl made by Jacob Boelen II of New York. Boelen was active from about 1750 to 1780 (Illus. 50). He conceived this bowl in the rococo style, taking a pyriform bowl, topping it with a curving domed cover and applying bands of elaborate *repoussé* ornament. Others matched the ornateness in comparable work.

Hot-water kettles were another form provided for the American tea table before the Revolution. The few surviving examples are quite elegant and appear to have been made by a craftsman well acquainted with English prototypes.

Mugs, canns, and tankards are traditional drinking vessels that were popular all through the eighteenth century. The plain flaring cylindrical mug with a simple handle is a form that reflects able craftsmanship more than style. An example made between 1720 and 1740

50. Sugar bowl. Jacob Boelen II (1733–84), 1760–75. The Metropolitan Museum of Art, Rogers Fund, 1939.

has subtle details at the lip and base (Illus. 51). Its maker, Benjamin Hiller, was working at the very beginning of the eighteenth century but continued to about 1745. While this mug is plain, it is well made. The form is more often seen in hastily worked pieces that lack the detailing Hiller applied.

Cann, or can, is the name given bulbous mugs that were significant from about 1730 to the end of the century. The shapes vary from squat and globular to elongated. The handles are more or less complex ear shapes that vary from piece to piece but most often have leaf ornament on top. Myer Myers' example of about 1760 has a more subtle curve than some earlier versions (Illus. 52). It resembles any number by more- and less-famous makers.

Tankards are another form that remained popular among Americans for most of the eighteenth century. London silversmiths seem to have made fewer than their American colleagues as interest in more

51. Cup. Benjamin Hiller (1687/8–1745), about 1720–40. Courtesy, The Henry Francis du Pont Winterthur Museum.

52. *Cann. Myer Myers (1723–95), about 1780. Ginsburg & Levy, Inc., New York.*

decorative tablewares increased. While London craftsmen dropped the simple tapering cylinder design, many Americans, particularly New Yorkers, did not. Those aware of changing fashion thinned down the squat body and added a band of molding around it about two-thirds of the way down from the top. Dome covers replaced the flat ones that had been common earlier. After 1760 fashion changed again, the cylinder was replaced by the bulbous body familiar on canns. Since tankards often hold as much as a quart or more, spouts were frequently added in the nineteenth century. The resulting form is rarely successful. When the spout has been removed and the piece restored, it is often possible to find the seams of the inset by careful inspection. This kind of restoration will make a piece less valuable although tankards are so rare today the most collectors are willing to settle for restored pieces.

Another problem is the fact that covers often were damaged and replaced. The account book of the New York silversmith Elias Pelletreau lists repair work and cover replacements more than once. While a new Pelletreau top might go unnoticed, a twentieth-century cover would be less attractive once discovered.

Flat-topped tankards with scroll-shaped thumbpieces in the squat proportions of late seventeenth-century London examples were made in New York at least as late as the 1760s. The tankard by Myer Myers has an elaborate cartouche framing the coat of arms of the

53. *Tankard. Myer Myers (1723–95). Collection of Philip H. Hammerslough.*

Livingston family which is obviously in the rococo style popular in the 1760s (Illus. 53). The first owners were Mary and Robert Livingston. He was the chancellor of New York who administered the oath to George Washington and was associated with Fulton in his steamboat venture. Samuel Tingley, a New York silversmith active from the 1760s to the end of the century used the domed cover with a plain tapering cylindrical body (Illus. 54). The more stylish design is seen in a tankard by Paul Revere (Illus. 55). Revere's fame is probably due as much to the Longfellow poem as to his ability as a silversmith. Despite the fact that his business interests were widespread, Paul Revere's shop produced many fine silver objects. He began working in the 1750s and was able to take over his father's shop in 1754 before he reached legal maturity. The tankard is outstanding with its steep domed cover topped by an elegant pine cone finial and the broad curving base band. The handle is simpler than that on a comparable London piece, which would have had an extra twist. Evidence that the most advanced designs were used by Americans from time to time is seen in the bulbous form of one by Philip Hulbert of Philadelphia. Hulbert died in 1764 so that he must have made

54. Tankard. Samuel Tingley (?), mentioned 1767. The Metropolitan Museum of Art, gift of Misses Mary Thurston Horn and Sarah Lawrence Horn, 1935.

55. Tankard. Paul Revere (1735–1818). The Metropolitan Museum of Art, bequest of A. T. Clearwater, 1933.

the tankard when the design was just being introduced in London (Illus. 56).

Dating American silver design is always difficult because though Americans could be in the latest fashion when they considered it desirable, they often preferred the old to the new. There is no consistency in what might be called a time lag. Apparently some patrons preferred old concepts to the new, but London design was well known in the colonies.

56. Tankard. Philip Hulbert (died 1764). Collection of Philip H. Hammerslough.

Baskets are a form that appear to be an ideal vehicle for rococo expression. Whether intended for bread, cake, or fruit is open to question, but whatever they held they were made to dazzle guests. The form was known in simple versions in London in the 1720s. English rococo examples are known from the 1730s and the 1740s, but the American rococo examples were products of the 1750s and 1760s and are very rare.

The two that have become well known because they are in public collections are by Daniel Christian Fueter and Myer Myers (Illus. 57, 58). Fueter used cast elements to create richly articulated details on the feet, the handle, and around the edge. These are in scroll, ribbon, shell, and human mask motifs characteristic of the rococo and restrained enough to be typically American. Myers relied on the piercing of the body, base, and handle to suggest the rococo. The undulating edge of the basket is another rococo motif, but neither the gadrooning nor the piercing could be related to the style.

Before as well as after the Revolution American silversmiths produced innumerable small boxes, rings, and other objects that might be sold at jewelers today. These frequently went unmarked so that it is difficult to distinguish the American products from the imports.

57. Bread basket. Daniel Christian Fueter (1720–85), about 1765. Courtesy, Museum of Fine Arts, Boston.

The snuffbox with the elaborate monogram has no mark, but it resembles one by Paul Revere (Illus. 59). Finding more of these small objects would be a good project for a serious collector. To avoid mistakes, it is important to compare documented eighteenth-century examples with more recent work to see how the thickness of details varies.

Spoons are a subject most easily discussed in a single place because there are a number of constants in their design which can be used to point up changes in conception that are significant. The form has a special appeal to many collectors because it is possible to acquire an extensive yet compact selection that may be considered a capsule history of silver design. Those interested in collecting marked silver should be able to find spoons by a great number of well-known makers to use to check the marks of more ambitious examples.

Spoons were often marked with a smaller touch than large holloware objects, but the style of the letters and symbols, if there were any, would be the same for both touches.

The earliest spoons by American makers are in the tradition of the plain Puritan spoons used in England at the beginning of the seventeenth century. These have round or elliptical bowls attached to straight handles that are square or rectangular in cross section. One ornate variation of an early form was made in New York, very likely as a funeral spoon that, according to tradition, was a gift for pallbearers. (Later examples are found with inscriptions of the name and date of death of the deceased.) Marked with the touch of P.G., a silversmith who has not been identified and who would appear to have worked in the vicinity of Albany, New York, the spoon has an unusual handle topped by a figure (Illus. 60). It is dated 1693 and represents the end of the baroque tradition.

58. *Cake basket. Myer Myers (1723–95), about 1765. The Metropolitan Museum of Art, purchase, 1954, Morris K. Jesup Fund.*

59. *Snuff box. Unidentified maker. Collection of Philip H. Hammer-slough.*

The 1690s marked the beginning of an era when more intimately scaled spoons were introduced to be used along with the ceremonial type that P.G. made. The new designs would seem to fit into the rococo tradition because of the scale, but the parts are not as integrated as they were to become after 1730 when the rococo reached the New World. A spoon made about 1695 by John Edwards appears to be much more delicate than the New York example (Illus. 61). The flatter and wider handle makes the bowl look smaller, and its curving lines which flair out at the end in a three-part curving tip have a special grace. The handle curves forward because it was designed to be placed on the table with its back up. The juncture of the

60. Spoon. P.G. (unidentified), Albany, 1693. Collections of Greenfield Village and the Henry Ford Museum, Dearborn, Michigan.

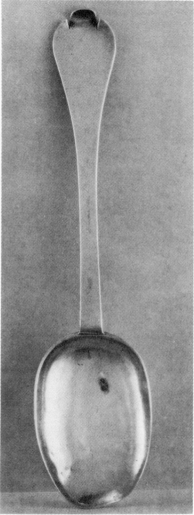

61. Trifid spoon. John Edwards (1661–1766), about 1695. Courtesy, The Henry Francis du Pont Winterthur Museum.

bowl and the handle on early spoons was often decorated since it was seen as guests sat down at a table.

There were many subtle variations of an essentially consistent form. One spoon made about 1700 by Jeremiah Dummer, for example, has a flatter bowl that widens close to the handle. The tip of its handle is curved but not cut (Illus. 62). By the 1730s handles were

62. *Wavy-end spoon. Jeremiah Dummer (1645–1718), about 1700. Courtesy, The Henry Francis du Pont Winterthur Museum.*

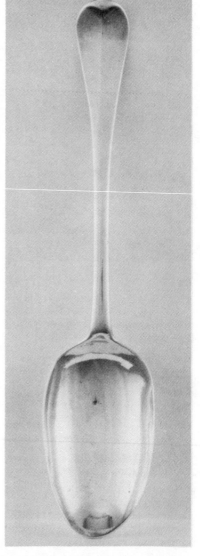

63. *Large serving spoon. Edward Winslow (1669–1753). Courtesy, The Henry Francis du Pont Winterthur Museum.*

thickened in designs conceived in three dimensions. The typical handle had a central ridge running from the end of the handle down a third or so to a point where it disappeared and the handle became very thin. A large spoon by Edward Winslow illustrated the charac-

64. Six forks. Myer Myers (1723–95), about 1760. Collection of Philip H. Hammerslough.

teristic emphatic curves of the form that remained popular from the 1730s to the 1760s (Illus. 63).

Whole services of flatware do not seem to have been made by Americans before the Revolution, but occasionally forks have turned up. There are early examples with the same kind of handles as the Edwards spoon. A set of small forks by Myer Myers have handles resembling those of the Winslow spoons (Illus. 64). Since the initials were engraved on the smooth backs, we can assume that forks were set on the table with the prongs curving down.

The introduction of a new style, neo-classicism, at about the time of the Revolution resulted in changes in the designs of spoons. The new style was characterized by a revival of specifically classical orna-

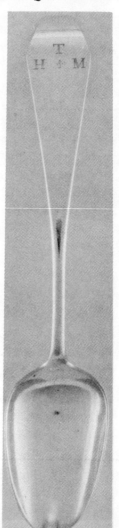

65. Bright-cut spoon. Joseph Richardson, Jr. (1752–1831), about 1790. Courtesy, The Henry Francis du Pont Winterthur Museum.

66. Coffin-handled spoon. Thomas Harland (1782–1849), about 1800. Courtesy, The Henry Francis du Pont Winterthur Museum.

ment and a greater delicacy. Spoon handles were flattened, the bowls elongated, and more engraved decoration was used. A spoon by

*67. Fiddle-shaped spoon. Thomas
Harland (1782–1849), about 1800.
Courtesy, The Henry Francis du
Pont Winterthur Museum.*

Joseph Richardson, Jr., of Philadelphia has a border of a repeating
deep V motif that is known as "Bright-cut" (Illus. 65). Another
popular post-Revolutionary spoon is plainer. Instead of the engraved
border, it is cut in a distinctive pattern that is thought to resemble a

coffin, earning the pattern the name "coffin-end" (Illus. 66). Thomas Harland made the coffin-end spoon about 1800.

The more complex handle design of the early nineteenth century brought more pleasant images to mind. The narrow stem broadened into a shape that is reminiscent of a violin case so the pattern is called "fiddleback." It was in fashion from about 1800 to 1850. Ordinarily plain or decorated with a shell at the tip, one very unusual example has a profile of Washington framed with laurel (Illus. 67). Thomas Harland, a Norwich, Connecticut, craftsman made matching forks to go with the Washington spoons some time before 1807 when he stopped working. Sets of spoons, knives, and forks were not popular until after 1815.

CHAPTER IV

The Neo-Classical
as an American Silver Style

The Revolution is the political event that occurred at about the same time as the radical change in design that resulted in the introduction of neo-classicism. There would seem to be a connection between the new political system and the new design since political essays of the time found models in governments of ancient Greece and Rome while designers sought inspiration in art of the same ancient sources as they reacted against the rococo style that had been in favor for several decades. The stylistic revolution was accompanied by technical innovations. There was an expansion of the size of many workshops and an increase in the amount of inexpensive work done. Many of the new designs were essentially simple so that they could be turned out more quickly and less expensively than the pre-Revolutionary. On the other hand, the demand for fine work continued and finely wrought silver of the period is well known. The major factor for the connoisseur to consider is the change in form and ornament that brought about the new classical style.

Neo-classicism is marked by two basic tendencies that reflect different approaches. First there is the reaction to the rococo, and then there is a rediscovery of the basis of Western style, the ancient Greco-Roman classical. The two are not easily separated. Up to the middle of the eighteenth century European design might best be characterized by terms that reveal its inventive use of classical motif.

Most popular ornament consisted of the leaf and various flowers and ribbons which can be traced to ancient art but had been adapted to suit the needs of a given moment. Rococo designs were furthest from the ancient models. When people tired of this style their reaction inspired a review of ancient sources. Rediscovery was stimulated by the newly awakened interest in history that had lured a few to recommence the archaeological research that had been neglected since the beginning of the Renaissance.

Probably the one American who can be associated with the new interest in the ancient world is Thomas Jefferson. His European travels included visits to ancient Roman monuments with an important French architect named Clerisseau. Clerisseau also had traveled with the Adam brothers, who have been credited with originating the neo-classical style. However, Jefferson was more sensitive to the changes in fashion than most Americans, and the new style was slow to gain acceptance in the new world. By the Eve of the Revolution, the 1770s, the new style was familiar to London silversmiths. Nevertheless, only one example—a presentation hot-water urn by Richard Humphreys—has been discovered so far to prove Americans worked in the neo-classical style in the 1770s. It is dated 1774, yet the most knowing connoisseur would have assumed it was from the 1790s if its history were not recorded. More typical is the much less ambitious circular or cylindrical teapot by Paul Revere (Illus. 68). The plain drum-shaped pot is simpler than anything rococo, as is characteristic of the new style. Revere used a gadrooned boarder and long straight spout to achieve a crisp, neat form that bears little obvious relationship to the classical in overall form. Nonetheless, the design is rather obviously different from the rococo and neo-classical.

Another teapot by Revere, bearing the date 1787, is a more complex expression of neo-classicism (Illus. 69). Oval with undulating sides, the punched and engraved borders are in a floral variation of the Greek key. The garland and frame around the monogram are more clearly classical but the essential element is the delicacy of both detail and line. Revere made both by seaming the parts together rather than the more elaborate process of raising.

The simplicity characteristic of post-Revolutionary work is also evident in a variety of small nearly functional objects. Boxes, for ex-

68. *Teapot. Paul Revere (1735–1818), about 1785. Collections of Greenfield Village and the Henry Ford Museum, Dearborn, Michigan.*

69. *Teapot. Paul Revere (1735–1818), 1787. Courtesy, Museum of Fine Arts, Boston, gift of estates of Misses Eunice McLellan and Frances Cordis Cruft.*

70. Presidential medal. 1789.
Courtesy, The Henry Francis du
Pont Winterthur Museum.

ample, were cut and soldered as economically as possible. Ovals, circles, square, and rectangles were most popular. Even the Indian Peace medals, made when the United States were first independent, are sheet silver cut in ovals and engraved, while earlier and later the medals were cast in more ambitious designs (Illus. 70).

Aside from the forms developed as neo-classical, the end of the eighteenth century was a time when functional forms best known in pottery or wood were made more important by being produced in silver. Barrel-shaped mugs are most frequently encountered among the work of English craftsmen, but then we find Paul Revere making

71. Pitcher. Paul Revere (1735–
1818), 1804. Courtesy, The Henry
Francis du Pont Winterthur Mu-
seum.

72. *Sugar bowl. Paul Revere (1735–1818), about 1770–1810. The Metropolitan Museum of Art, bequest of A. T. Clearwater, 1933.*

pitchers that duplicate the form of the pottery mugs imported from Liverpool (Illus. 71). Modeled after inexpensive creamware examples, the lines are simple enough to appeal to anyone who admired the new approach. Most important are the more elaborate examples of neo-classical work. Going back to work by Paul Revere, a sugar bowl by him in the form of a footed basket illustrates the new approach well (Illus. 72). The form is crisply detailed because the sides are widely fluted and the decoration is delicately scaled engraving. The tassels and garlands of drapery engraved around the piece are typically neo-classical. The wide fluting adds to the brightness of objects by adding to the reflections on the surface of any given example.

Revere was just one of many craftsmen who produced silver at the end of the century, but his work is relatively well preserved. More of his silver has survived than that of his many competitors. The fact that a few pieces bearing Revere marks have the name J. Austin—another silversmith—stamped over Revere's name suggests that his shop was large enough to turn out work for others.

Conservatism is a recurring factor in late eighteenth-century design. There are many instances in the 1780s and '90s when a rococo form was only mildly modified to suit the neo-classical. The coffee-pot by John Vernon of New York has moldings around the base and lip that are too delicate for rococo efforts (Illus. 73). The pear shape has become a bit bulbous and the spout very straight to update the piece and make it more suitable for a 1790 table than one a few decades earlier.

73. Coffeepot. John Vernon (working 1787–1815), about 1790. The Metropolitan Museum of Art, bequest of A. T. Clearwater, 1933.

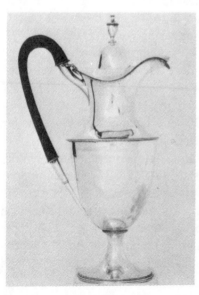

74. Sugar urn with cover. Daniel van Voorhis (1751–1824), 1790–1800. The Metropolitan Museum of Art, bequest of A. T. Clearwater, 1933.

75. Hot-water pot. Van Voorhis (1751–1824) and Schanck (working 1791–92). The Metropolitan Museum of Art, bequest of Charles Allen Munn, 1924.

76. Sugar bowl. Van Voorhis (1751–1824) and Schanck (working 1791–92). The Museum of the City of New York, gift of Mrs. de Peyster Hosmer.

For the innovative silversmith early neo-classicism was more often a matter of choosing proportions and details echoing the ancient than of adapting shapes identifiable as classical. However, a number of the early neo-classical covered urns are based on ancient models. The urn was useful as either a sugar bowl or a teapot, but it was not used consistently.

Daniel van Voorhis was first a Philadelphia and then a New York craftsman who entered into a number of different partnerships between 1780 and 1800. One sugar urn he made is crisp, plain, and classical (Illus. 74). The smooth surface is relieved by borders of beading, and a pineapple finial tops the whole thing. A hot-water pot by Van Voorhis and Schanck is closely related to the sugar urn, and the difference in the finial shows how subtle variations could be introduced (Illus. 75). Another example by the partners is a sugar bowl that is squat and elliptical with extensive engraving (Illus. 76). Possibly more unusual because the piece appears to have been cut out of a sheet and soldered in panels, the general outline is classical but the straight lines of the panels are not. The decoration, engraved details of shields, oval medallions, and feathery garlands, make up a most characteristic repertory of neo-classical ornament. Van Voorhis produced this while working with Schanck between 1791 and 1792.

77. *Tea set. Joseph Lownes (1754–1820), about 1785. Ginsburg &
Levy, Inc., New York.*

From all indications in early records Van Voorhis was successful
and good. In partnership with others and alone he maintained shops
in which he sold his own work as well as imports. As an expert craftsman he was less interested in innovation than supplying the needs
of his customers. What bears his mark is not very different from
work by his competitors, but the same statement would apply to any
of the silversmiths active on the American scene.

Joseph Lownes of Philadelphia made a tea set for the DeCosta
family of the same city that might have included the sugar urn by
Van Voorhis, the design is so similar (Illus. 77). On the other hand,
if we were to review all the known work by Lownes, we could find
amazing variety. He made bulbous mugs and barrel-like ribbed tankards, candlesticks in a distinctive Empire style, and tea sets almost
matching the fluted pot by Revere.

Tea sets were popular after the Revolution. Ordinarily they included one or two pots, a waste bowl, sugar urn, container for milk
or cream, and sometimes even a tea caddy. In the early nineteenth

78. Presentation urn. Joseph Lownes (1754–1820), 1799. Collection of Philip H. Hammerslough.

century tea became more important as a social ceremony, and examining the objects used, it would seem that tea parties increased in size since pots got bigger and large hot-water urns more common.

Urns made as presentation pieces for people who had performed heroic deeds are better known in the nineteenth than the eighteenth century. Many of these were given by insurance companies or ship owners to the person who saved a cargo from robbers or fire. One of the more unusual examples appears to be earlier in style than most (Illus. 78). Joseph Lownes made it as a gift from the Marine Insurance Office to Captain William Anderson. Although no date appears on the urn itself, there is a good chance that the event it commemorates occurred in 1799. The lightness of the proportions and the delicacy of the engraved decoration and the bands of molding are ele-

79. Tea caddy. Probably John Walraven (working 1792–1814), touchmark Baltimore, 1805. Ginsburg & Levy, Inc., New York.

ments that make the piece look even earlier than 1799. Amusingly enough, Lownes did not follow classical prototypes for this urn as well as he did for the tea set.

A splendid tea caddy made in Baltimore about 1805 is in a characteristic shape, a six-inch-high box with curving sides (Illus. 79). The broad fluting and the crisp engraving are in proper neo-classical spirit. The Baltimore silversmith responsible, probably John Walraven, was evidently capable of the highest quality work.

Cake or bread baskets in the neo-classical style were often more simply put together than earlier models. Elaborate cast ornaments were dropped with piercing and engraving more than adequate substitutes (Illus. 80). Simeon Bayley of New York artfully seamed and soldered sheets of silver cut to form an elegant basket. The job took much less time than Fueter's basket mentioned earlier, but the results are very successful.

Bowls were a popular presentation gift in the eighteenth century. Examples are found with inscriptions that commemorate events as disparate as horse races and political meetings. A bowl by Isaac Hutton of Albany might pass for pre-Revolutionary if one did not take careful account of the moldings around both the base and the lip (Illus. 81). Made as an award of the Society for the Promotion of Useful Arts in 1811, its lines reveal it to be a subtly up-dated version of a traditional form. Hutton took about the same approach in

80. Cake basket. Simeon A. Bayley (working 1785–97). The Museum of the City of New York, gift of George Elsworth Dienscombe.

making a caster (Illus. 82). It follows a basically eighteenth-century design, but the narrowness of the bands around the base, the shoulder, the mouth, and the top are telltales of its later date. The flatness at the base and the shoulder are other details that indicate the caster was made in about 1800 rather than 1750. On the other hand, columnar sticks by Hutton are the ultimate expression of the neo-classical. Plain, save for the flutes on the columns, they are fashionably Empire (Illus. 83).

A cannon-ball-shaped covered punch bowl is a part of one of the more unusual presentation sets given by the citizens of Baltimore after the War of 1812 (Illus. 84). The recipient was George Armistead, the officer in charge of the soldiers who defended Fort McHenry while Francis Scott Key was writing "The Star-Spangled

81. Bowl. Isaac Hutton (1767–1855). The Metropolitan Museum of Art, gift of Earl D. Babst, 1953, in memory of Alice Edwina Uhl Babst.

82. Pepper caster. Isaac Hutton (1767–1855), about 1800. The Metropolitan Museum of Art, bequest of A. T. Clearwater, 1933.

83. Pair of candlesticks. Isaac Hutton (1767–1855), 1800–25. The Metropolitan Museum of Art, bequest of A. T. Clearwater, 1933.

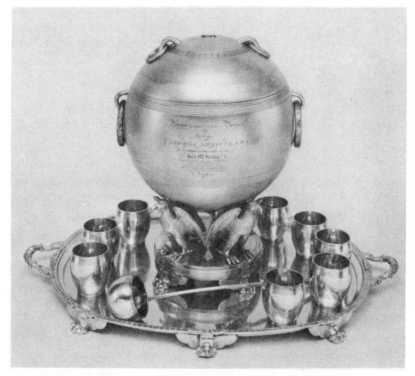

84. Punch set. Bowl by Thomas Fletcher and Sidney Gardiner, Philadelphia, cups by Andrew E. Warner, Baltimore, about 1815.

Banner." The set's perfect Southern spirit seems to explain why it is for punch rather than tea. The cannon ball has been dressed up with such classical elements as wreathes for handles, eagles to form the stand that supports the ball, and winged lion feet on which the bottom tray stands. Barrel-shaped cups were used with it. The punch bowl was made by Thomas Fletcher and Sidney Gardiner who produced any number of impressive presentation urns. The citizens of Baltimore were either patriotic or economical because they ordered the barrel-shaped cups from a local craftsman, Andrew Warner. The set is very unusual. It suggests how early nineteenth-century classicism was tempered by an interest in useful forms. Barrel mugs and cups were a popular English design of the late eighteenth century.

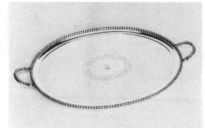

85. Tea set tray. Andrew E. Warner (1786-1870). Collection of Philip H. Hammerslough.

Andrew Warner was one of Baltimore's abler and more prolific craftsmen. He produced elegant work in classical designs in the early nineteenth century when Baltimore was the scene of the production of the richest efforts in all the decorative arts. Baltimore craftsmen tapped the latest London sources for the newest in furniture as well as silver. A tea tray by Warner has a border of beads that are in full relief and an ideal foil for the overall pattern of punched stars that cover the surface (Illus. 85). This punchwork was used by other silversmiths, as, for example, Samuel Kirk.

Chamber candlesticks with holders are not seen often in silver so that the pair by Andrew Warner are particularly important (Illus. 86). The tray on which the candleholder rests was designed for safety when walking with lighted candles. The contrast of the simple holder

86. Pair of chamber candlesticks. Andrew E. Warner (1786-1870). Collection of Philip H. Hammerslough.

to the ornate tray is striking, and the cast border is yet another note of elegance on this utilitarian form.

Andrew Warner varied designs to suit the taste of his patrons. A salver commissioned in 1817 as a gift to Stephen Decatur by the citizens of Baltimore has a thick border in broad relief with the Leviathan from the Bible as its main motif (Illus. 87). The design is heavier than that of most of the more familiar Warner pieces.

Occasionally Baldwin Gardiner is confused with Sidney Gardiner who was a partner of Thomas Fletcher in both Boston and Philadel-

87. *Salver. Andrew E. Warner (1786–1870), 1817. The Metropolitan Museum of Art, bequest of A. T. Clearwater, 1933.*

phia. Baldwin Gardiner worked in New York producing silver between about 1814 and 1838, often using designs similar to those of Fletcher and Gardiner. Two trays marked B. Gardiner indicate that he also worked in the light neo-classical style (Illus. 88). While not a pair, since the engraved borders differ, the monograms on the two trays are the same. The depth of the outer rim and the curving moldings around it are the same on both. Both were examples of the neo-classicism in fashion right after the Revolution.

The heavier, more classical phase of neo-classicism took hold on the American scene after 1810, but it was known before that. Neoclassicism had evolved as a style characterized by a revival of the use of classical ornament in forms that were relatively simple. Rectangles, squares, circles, and ovals dominated with decoration that was small-scaled and delicate. Some objects were made in shapes familiar to the ancient world, but most often the forms were contemporary invention.

Using the ancient forms as the model for the design of fashionable objects became more popular at the beginning of the nineteenth century. The occasional efforts at reviving ancient classical forms in

88. Two trays. Baldwin Gardiner (working 1814–38). Ginsburg &
Levy, Inc., New York.

the eighteenth century were not influential until the very end of the
eighteenth century when Napoleon's designers, Percier and Fon-
taine, introduced furnishings of every kind in designs based on an-

89. Candlestick. John Lynch (1761–1840), about 1795. Courtesy, The Henry Francis du Pont Winterthur Museum.

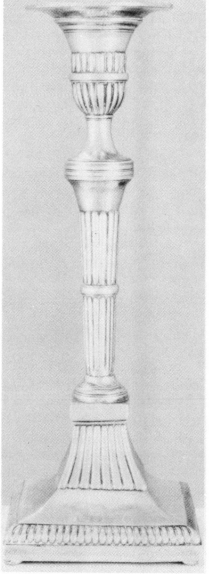

cient models. By 1810 the so-called Empire style (after the Emperor Napoleon) had caught on everywhere from Paris to Moscow and Detroit, but it did not necessarily displace the lighter less archeological neo-classical, and both phases of the style were significant until about 1820.

A fluted urn and pedestal-shaped candlestick illustrates an early expression of the archeological neo-classicism (Illus. 89). The basic design might have been dated later if the mark were not indicative of the fact that John Lynch of Baltimore stamped it before 1800. Lynch used a plain I L mark which appears only on his early work. The design is not very different from London work of about 1790.

French influence was always important but it increased when the Revolution drove many craftsmen out of France to England and the United States. The French emigrants were among the innovators, so that we find them leading the silversmiths to the richest Empire-style designs.

The new aspect of neo-classicism is illustrated by forms that look heavy and ornament that derives from the ancient. Anthony Rasch, a French emigrant working in Philadelphia, used a serpent as the handle and a ram's head for the spout of a squat but graceful sauce-boat (Illus. 90). Although there are French prototypes for the Rasch sauceboats, the sparing use of ornament is characteristic of the American touch.

An equally important example of the French influence is by a sometime partner of Rasch, Simon Chaudron (Illus. 91). This two-spout punch pot is relatively heavy in its proportions, and it has cast ornament fairly large-scaled as is typical of the Empire style. The form and the decoration are both rare, but they suggest the approach that became important in the nineteenth century.

More conservative but not less Empire in spirit are a pair of sauce-boats that have only leaf and beading decoration (Illus. 92). The work of Eoff and Shepherd of New York, these sauceboats display proportions about the same as those on the Rasch example. Here the leaf is heavy and in high relief to show off the fine quality of the detailing.

By the 1830s there were any number of shops that sold more silver than they made. Marquand & Co. was one establishment that commissioned work and one pitcher on record bears the mark of Baldwin Gardiner as well as the statement "Manufactured by Marquand &

90. *Sauceboat. A. Rasch and Co., about 1810. The Metropolitan Museum of Art, Sansbury Mills Fund, 1959.*

91. *Punch pot. Simon Chaudron (working 1798–1814). The Metropolitan Museum of Art, gift of Mr. and Mrs. Marshall P. Blankarn, 1966.*

Co., N.Y." The shape is standard for late Empire examples with bands of anthemions used as borders.

Empire-style silver is fairly easy to find because it was made in quantity all over the United States. All the large cities had shops making silver and even some smaller towns had attracted working silversmiths.

The more elegant silversmiths in the large cities produced elaborate work, but they and countless craftsmen in smaller communities supplied the demand for popular-priced work by making simple holloware. Tea sets, mugs, and a selection of other small objects for the table were made of thin sheet silver with minimal decoration.

The inexpensive examples are frequently stripped-down versions of the more elaborate. Basic designs of the expensive are often the same as those of the inexpensive, but the ornament is omitted when price was a factor. Whatever the price, the classical urn is the model for the various parts of a tea set. While the inspiration for early and late examples was similar, proportions differed. The characteristic 1815–40 teapot was heavier in proportion than the 1790–1815 example. Wide reeding and relief ornament replaced the shallow broad flutes and delicate engraving common on the earlier work. The scope of late pieces is broad and the collector should be prepared to encounter surprises.

92. *Pair of sauceboats. Eoff and Shepherd (working 1824–38). Ginsburg & Levy, Inc., New York.*

Finding a lion's head spout is unexpected on an otherwise standard teapot. It was used by the early nineteenth-century New York silversmith Garrett Eoff on a teapot on lion's paw feet (Illus. 93). Rich relief leaf ornament was applied to the spout, the end of the legs, and the dome-shaped cover. While the decoration is characteristic of the period, the pot is an unusual design.

Squat shapes on round bases or small ball feet were much more common for the Empire style. A tea set by N. Taylor and Company of New York is simple but fine (Illus. 94). The head of the company was Najah Taylor who had begun his career in Connecticut, and it was not listed in the directories after 1818. The undulating

93. *Teapot. Garrett Eoff (1785–1858). The Metropolitan Museum of Art, bequest of A. T. Clearwater, 1933.*

94. *Tea set. N. Taylor & Co. (working in New York 1808–17). The Museum of the City of New York, bequest of Gabrielle di Cesnola Delcambre.*

vine motif that had been chased on a band was then applied to each of the pieces in the set around the base and an upper area. These bands may have been made by specialists since occasionally the work of two or more silversmiths have the same decorative bands.

A tea set on plain ball feet by Forbes of New York is an interesting variation (Illus. 95). Forbes was more elegant than many of his competitors in his choice of ornament. The vine band is flat but wide and sets off both the completely plain body and the narrow, busier floral bands that were applied around the bases, on the rim of the creamer and covers of the sugar bowl and teapot. The dolphin handles represent the use of an extremely popular motif that was also found on Empire furniture, ceramics, and glass.

William B. Heyer's teapot is the simpler version (Illus. 96). Heyer omitted all decoration except the two narrow bands of gadrooning. Heyer sometimes added bands of stamped ornament. Agricultural items, including farmhouses and beehives were included in one of the bands of relief Heyer and a few of his competitors used.

Empire-style classical forms were important as late as the middle of the nineteenth century. The later examples may be very much like earlier models, but occasionally it is easy to distinguish later exam-

95. Tea set. C: and J. W. Forbes (1810–19). Ginsburg & Levy, Inc., New York.

96. Teapot. William B. Heyer (working 1798–1827). The Metropolitan Museum of Art, bequest of A. T. Clearwater, 1933.

97. Sugar bowl. Robert and William Wilson (working 1825–46). The Metropolitan Museum of Art, bequest of A. T. Clearwater, 1933.

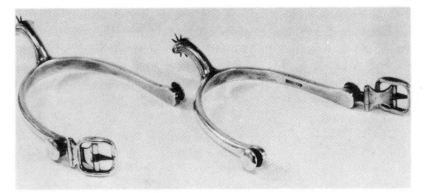

98. *Pair of spurs. Paul Revere (1735–1818). The Cleveland Museum of Art, gift of Hollis French.*

99. *Funnel. Unidentified maker. Collection of Philip H. Hammerslough.*

ples. The sugar bowl made by Robert and William Wilson in the 1840s has a high relief garland that resembles those found on the later rococo revival examples (Illus. 97). The tall shape is a lightened version of the squat models. It was part of the reaction to the Empire after three decades of its prominence.

The use of silver for unusual objects was popular in the early nineteenth century. Spurs are just one of a variety of forms encountered (Illus. 98). The spurs by Paul Revere are plain, but their solidity is characteristic of their period when solid craftsmanship was particularly important. Later examples are often made more flimsily.

The number of nineteenth-century functional objects made of silver that are known keeps growing as new forms are discovered. Funnels (Illus. 99), marrow spoons, tea scoops, butter measures, tubes for distilling spirits, and even bidets have turned up. A bidet by a New York silversmith was discovered in Cuba just as Castro was taking over. Considering the range of what has been found, it is difficult to predict what will be turning up next. Utilitarian forms were quite popular when the emphasis was on the classical.

CHAPTER V

Victorian (or Nineteenth Century) Is Different

Collectors once restricted their activities to seeking out work made before 1830. They considered that to be the end of the era of craftsmanship, and thought that well-designed handsome pieces were excessively rare after 1830. Now there is a growing interest in work of every period since early silver is beyond the reach of the pocketbooks of many who are fascinated enough by the metal to want to collect anyway. They are willing to investigate the once-scorned Victorian era, dating about 1830 to 1900, and to learn about the variety of design significant during those seven decades.

At first glance it is obvious that objects made in the Victorian era differ from those made earlier. These differences suggest that both technological and sociological changes in the United States affected design and must be considered to develop an understanding of nineteenth-century silver.

The most challenging aspect of nineteenth-century design is the ugliness of some of it. Most of us find it easy to like anything eighteenth century, and even if we prefer the simple to the most elaborate output, we can respect the merits of what we would prefer not having for our own. Nineteenth-century work, on the other hand, is apt to arouse the hostility of a potential collector, who is often sure he knows where the designer went wrong. Whether it is the heavy relief ornament of the 1850s or the light linear engraving of the 1880s, the twentieth-century connoisseur often has more of a problem appreciating these than he would have with earlier examples.

Some estheticians explain this negative reaction by saying the period is too close to be appreciated; others believe the negativism to be correct because conditions had changed to make the situation ripe for the beginning of bad design. The pure opportunistic commercialism that spawned bad design had not existed before the end of the eighteenth century, but it has been rampant from that point on. Judges for a good design exhibition today would show no more than about 10 per cent of what was manufactured, and in the middle of the nineteenth century similar groups would probably have selected about half of what was available.

The most striking difference between the cultures of the nineteenth century and the eighteenth century is in the expanded demand for fashionably designed objects. The eighteenth-century consumer was satisfied with more or less styleless objects at low cost, and we would see that simple mugs and tankards of the eighteenth century are often difficult to date. While certain quantities of simple wares were produced in the nineteenth century, much more effort was made to keep up with fashion. The nineteenth-century demand for luxury and for elaborate decoration came at every level. From the kitchen to the parlor, and from the homes of the most affluent to the simplest households, fashionable work was in demand. This demand differed from those of earlier eras in that more or less obvious adaptations of fashionable design had been the basis of charming popular efforts in the eighteenth century (and they continued to be important in rural areas where fashion was unknown). However, in the nineteenth century it was equally elaborate work in close imitations of precious metals that were demanded. A series of inventions that made it possible to mass-produce elaborate decorative metals that resembled silver helped manufacturers supply the new needs.

Silver manufacturing was completely transformed in the course of the century as the small shops of able craftsmen lost ground to the large factories in the production of both sterling and plated silver. For the collector, the most confusing aspect of Victorian silver is attempting to set up appropriate standards to decide if a design was successful originally. Obviously, the esthetic of the nineteenth century differed from that of the eighteenth century. Within the period there were changes in taste that caused variations in basic forms. One can find squat forms at one moment and elongated ones at another. There were times when decoration in high relief was fashionable and times when flat ornament was in demand.

The demand for fashionable wares in every price category in the nineteenth century differed from similar demands earlier. Before 1800 most people who wanted inexpensive decorative wares settled for pewter, but, having first been agreeable to a brighter version of pewter called Britannia, the public soon held out for silver plate. Also, the Victorian buyer wanted elaborate decoration at every price level. The invention of electroplating made it possible to cover base metal with silver.

Plated silver had been developed in the eighteenth century when thin outer sheets of silver were combined with a center sheet of copper. The most famous center for plating was Sheffield, but by the end of the eighteenth century the large Birmingham factories produced the greatest quantities of the plated silver. Birmingham manufacturers working on a relatively large scale produced a variety of plated silver forms. A few American manufacturers used plated silver in the early nineteenth century, but more often imported plate was offered. Since pewter was meeting with some sales resistance, even when improved and called Britannia, in the 1820s a more adequate substitute called German or nickel-silver was introduced. It is an alloy of nickel, copper, and zinc that looks more like silver than Britannia did. However, it was harder and more difficult to spin nickel-silver than Britannia.

Silver plate was the only really adequate substitute for silver, and it was the development of electroplating that made it possible for plating to be used by the many factories producing substitutes for silver. The process of causing a deposit of silver to adhere to a base-metal surface with the aid of a battery had been developed in 1828 by the English manufacturer Elkington. A Philadelphian, John O. Mead, is credited with introducing the process in the United States. According to an account of Philadelphia manufactures by E. T. Freedly, Mead had acquired the key battery in 1837 and was able to plate silver electrically by 1839. Mead joined with William and Asa Rogers to manufacture silver plate in Hartford, Connecticut, in about 1845, but that partnership was terminated when Roger Bros. was founded in 1847.

The early history of plating is not properly documented. While there are claims that the first important plated pieces were made in the 1840s, the catalogues of the Massachusetts Charitable Association Fairs list silver plate as early as 1839 when it was exhibited by Jones, Lows and Ball as well as Harris & Stanwood. By the 1840s the list of those making silver plate was larger, but it included several, such as Jones, Lows and Poor (the new name for the firm), that also made sterling silver. In 1850 silver plate was made by a number of companies that had begun as Britannia manufacturers, but each of the larger makers produced Britannia and nickel-silver along with the plated wares, and in 1876 the Philadelphia Centennial Exhibition catalogues included work in the base metals along with silver and silver plate.

An awareness of the base-metal output may be helpful to the collector who might otherwise be overly optimistic about finding a blackened object that could be silver.

Silver plate was constantly improved over the years. Marks of triple and quadruple plating are common on wares made after 1860. Many of the manufacturers suggested the hardiness of their product by implying it had three or four layers of silver applied.

As the silversmith's workshops expanded and the techniques he used changed, the character of his work also underwent profound transformations. The role of the designer in early work is not clear. Most often the craftsmen adapted or copied from a model. Although the most important silversmiths of London or Paris might have employed detailed drawings prepared for them, the slight evidence of American designing reveals craftsmen executed not-too-original drawings of pieces that they were to make. There is no clear evidence of the background of the designers responsible for the molds that were to become important for casting and stamping in the later work. Obviously, the designers reflected the taste of their time, and each style was succeeded by one that satisfied new interests and was a reaction to what went before. In the major shops design was taken seriously, and we find that Tiffany credited its designers with their achievements. Edward Moore, whose family had owned the silver plant taken over by Tiffany, is known to have been responsible for significant designs executed with all possible skill. One of the Tiffany designs of the 1880s was adapted for plated wares at the International Silver Company factory. The silver-plate manufacturer very simply used the sterling piece as a model and changed what was necessary.

In addition to the differences between silver and silver plate that are a matter of the basic values of the materials used, there are differences in design that reflect taste. The sterling is apt to be the more subtle or more complex, while the plate is a more popular rendition. The plate has to glitter more, its decoration has to be more ostentatious. In a sense, the plated pieces are designed to appeal to the more popular level, and often the results would seem akin to folk art in the way they can be appreciated best by those who like design obvious.

Collectors should remember that nineteenth-century silver varied in quality as well as approach. The plated wares that are more common are sometimes a lot less pleasing. They were designed by manufacturers trying to guess what was salable. Occasionally they simply copied more fashionable efforts but then were forced to compromise by modifying ornament to make it possible to produce the piece at the right cost. Often these modifications are not all bad, and the cheap copy can be most attractive. It depends upon the way a design is changed. Those who knew how to reduce the degree of ornament without making a piece look stripped down produced significant wares. Buying such work is not costly, and it can be fun to follow the trends of the nineteenth century in work that is moderately ornate. To follow nineteenth-century design it is essential that the finer wares be traced first. At this point it isn't possible to track down all the popular designs of the nineteenth century, but the finer wares that were publicized and documented in their displays at the major international exhibitions can be shown as illustrations of a history of silver design. While the popular wares do not follow the evolution step by step, they were made by manufacturers who were aware of changing fashion.

CHAPTER VI

Revival Styles: 1830–70

In the 1820s designers began experimenting with using motifs from a variety of historic styles to create something new to replace the dominant Empire style. Not all were used with equal enthusiasm, but the Gothic, the "Elizabethan," the Louis XIV (which was really rococo and Louis XV), and the Renaissance were all mentioned in contemporary essays on style as proper sources of inspiration for new design. The new forms developed were required to fill the needs and please the taste of the time, but ornamentation was selected from an extensive repertory garnered by studying historic models. This method introduced in the 1820s was still used in the 1870s, although proportions changed and forms varied. Decorative objects were conceived in one of the several styles in fashion at the moment, and the very word style took on a new meaning in that it referred to the period from which models for decoration and ornament were selected rather than the whole or deeper concept of design.

As far as we can tell today, silversmiths were not as broad in their view of design as architects and furniture designers. Although there is no book to describe the silversmith's approach during the nineteenth century, examples of the 1830s and 1840s that turn up are generally either Empire, Gothic, or rococo. On the other hand, a book by A. J. Downing, *The Architecture of Country Houses*, published about 1840, suggests ways of furnishing homes and recom-

100. Communion set. Francis W. Cooper (working 1840–68), about 1845. Collections of Greenfield Village and the Henry Ford Museum, Dearborn, Michigan.

mends that styles be used one at a time. According to it, a single room was better looking if everything in it was in the same style.

The few early examples of the Gothic revival silver that have survived were used originally in churches. Typical is a communion set by Francis W. Cooper of New York of about 1845 now at the Henry Ford Museum (Illus. 100). Cooper's paten and ewer are based on medieval models, but the decoration has been modified radically. In the medieval examples enamel colors and applied wire might have been used for ornamentation (as it was in more elaborate revival pieces), but here it is simply handsome engraving of the simplest variety. Gothic services of flatware were not made until the 1870s, but it would not be surprising to turn up an 1845–50 tea set since the Gothic arch is found on ceramic water pitchers and spittoons of that period.

The precise date of any change in style on the American scene is difficult to determine. Documented examples have to be evaluated because a single manifestation of a new style is not proof that a change has occurred.

The rococo revival was introduced to English and French craftsmen in the 1820s and a few isolated pieces suggest Americans were aware of the new designs. Since Empire-style silver is common, it must be assumed that the rococo was slow to be accepted.

Besides being a simple and obvious reaction to the classical Empire, the rococo revival probably appealed to those aware of its importance in the eighteenth century. Political problems in France had revived the hopes of royalists attempting to reinstate the Bourbon dynasty. Along with this renewed interest in a past way of life, great eighteenth-century Parisian court furnishings were bringing high prices on the market and attracting the attention of connoisseurs and craftsmen. One might see this as related to the Art Deco revival in the 1960s, when objects less than forty years old were coveted at high prices in answer to needs stimulated by a wave of nostalgia.

The London silversmith Paul Storr, known for producing the most elaborate silver in the early nineteenth century, was making rococo revival pieces by 1810. His work was sometimes close enough to the eighteenth-century models to be considered survival rather than

101. Tea service. J. and I. Cox, about 1850. Brooklyn Museum Collection.

revival, but more often rich relief ornament in rococo motifs were employed on larger and heavier forms than those popular in the first phase of the rococo. By the 1830s the rococo was a revival style significant on both sides of the Atlantic. In some instances the rococo was used in combination with the accepted Empire style, but more often new designs followed the rococo esthetic which involved squat curving shapes embellished with floral scroll and leaf motifs.

A combination of Empire and rococo revival was employed in the design of a tea set made by J. and I. Cox of New York in about 1850 (Illus. 101). The broad fluting is a classical element in pieces that are squat and asymmetrical in the best rococo manner. The floral finials and curving handles embellished with leaves and scrolls emphasize the rococo in a fairly simple way.

The pitcher made by Bard and Lamont of Philadelphia in 1841 is an even more surprising expression of two styles (Illus. 102). The fact that it was made as a presentation piece given to an abolitionist

102. Pitcher. Bard and Lamont (working 1840–?), 1841. Detroit Institute of Art.

103. *Sugar bowl. William Forbes (working 1828–50), 1841. Collections of Greenfield Village and the Henry Ford Museum, Dearborn, Michigan.*

lawyer adds extra interest to the basically classical urnlike form. The borders are in a delicate leaf pattern as characteristic of the Empire as the winged lion's paw feet that support its stand. The leaf-and-scroll design around the middle of the piece are in the spirit of the curving handle.

Coincidentally contemporary, a sugar bowl of 1841 by William Forbes of New York has cast pierced rococo leaf-and-scroll work on the main portion of the bowl (Illus. 103). This bowl is marked with the name of the retailer, Ball, Tompkins and Black, as well as the silversmith. As ambitious as the decoration is, the decorative elements have been assembled simply and, since the ornament is cast rather than executed more delicately by hammering out each detail, there is a less finished quality to the results. The difference between the nineteenth- and the eighteenth-century approach is emphasized here, but generally the former is executed with a heavier hand. The success of the nineteenth-century effort is dependent upon how consistent the designer is. Forbes understood the shortcomings of his technique and did not attempt to fake detailing in any way.

Another key example of rococo revival design is the teakettle and stand by Edward Lownes who worked in Philadelphia between 1817 and 1834 (Illus. 104). Lownes repeats an eighteenth-century model known better in London than Philadelphia but there is an important distinction between his and the earlier versions. Lownes' characteristically nineteenth-century touch is in the way the ornament is overemphasized. The gadrooning and the leaf patterns are deeper and attract more attention than they would on an eighteenth-century piece.

Gold and gold-plated silver were an extravagance that was encountered in the mid-nineteenth century. Part of the American exhibit at the London Crystal Palace exhibition of 1851 was a gold tea set made by John Chandler Moore for Ball, Tompkins and Black of New York in the rococo style. Edwin Stebbins and Co. made a less elaborately ornamented tea set for the Crocker family between about 1840 and 1850 (Illus. 105). The decoration is limited to bands of leaves that are Empire, but the curving handles are rococo as are the forms. A relatively simple pair of goblets in the

104. Teakettle on stand. Edward Lownes (active 1817–34). Courtesy, The Henry Francis du Pont Winterthur Museum.

105. Tea set (gold-plated silver). Edwin Stebbins & Co. (1840–50). Collections of Greenfield Village and the Henry Ford Museum, Dearborn, Michigan.

rococo style were given to the State Department collection by Philip Hammerslough. These goblets were made of gold by Wood and Hughes of New York and suggest that precious metal may have been used more than is understood today.

The variety of rococo revival design was extensive. Some pieces, such as the Lownes teakettle, were fairly close to the eighteenth-century models. Others, were radically different. Water pitchers were not used much in the eighteenth century but they became very popular in the nineteenth century. Rococo revival examples are new forms that tend to be based on Empire-style models. A pair that were made about 1845 for Ball, Tompkins and Black of New York have Empire bands of ornament along with rococo decoration. Handles are particularly elegant prominent flowers in relief. Scroll, shells, and flowers are engraved and chased on the main part of the body in a way that is more symmetrical than would be expected.

Variations in quality are too seldom noted in nineteenth-century wares. Since inexpensive work was made in quantity, it was not usual to find decoration that was executed too quickly. Among the most impressive examples of the rococo are those by John Chandler Moore whose shop merged with Tiffany in 1868. Moore's tea set presented to Marshall Lefferts in 1867 has elaborate *repoussé* decoration in a grape motif (Illus. 106, 107). Individual pieces are free interpretations of the eighteenth-century models, but most important, the decoration is rendered with an emphasis on detail that is distinctively characteristic of the nineteenth century. In the eighteenth century fruit, scrolls, and shells were hardly recognizable when used as motifs of elaborate ornament, but the best mid-nineteenth-century craftsmen were concerned with realistic rendering. Moore's grapes are no less carefully executed than those in a still life

106. *Teakettle. John Chandler Moore (working 1832–51), 1850. The Metropolitan Museum of Art, gift of Mrs. F. R. Lefferts, 1969.*

107. *Creamer. John Chandler Moore (working 1832–51), 1850. The Metropolitan Museum of Art, gift of Mrs. F. R. Lefferts, 1969.*

108. Tea set. Charters, Cann, and Dunn, about 1850. Collections of Greenfield Village and the Henry Ford Museum, Dearborn, Michigan.

of the period. Mediocre work, on the other hand, has detail rendered with much less care.

Charters, Cann, and Dunn were New York silversmiths active at mid-century. The tea service they made for James Polk is less elegant than Moore's, but the grapes and leaves on the handles suggest this was a special effort (Illus. 108). Squat forms with paneled sides were common for teapots and sugar bowls (A set illustrated in the catalogue of the London Crystal Palace exhibition of 1851 by Broadhead & Atkin is similar.) *The repoussé* flowers and scrolls are motifs frequently encountered on work of the period. Details are complex, perspective has been employed, but there is less of a sense of realism than in the decoration of the Moore set.

By the 1860s American Britannia manufacturers were working in the rococo style also. They made tea sets in silver plate as well as

No.		Set of 6 pieces.	10 half pint Coffee.	6 half pint Tea.	5 half pint Tea.	Sugar.	Cream.	Slop.
Chased,	4100	$37.50	$9.50	$7.50	$7.00	$5.00	$4.50	$4.00
Chased,	*4200	39.00	10.00	8.00	7.50	5.00	4.50	4.00
Engine,	*4200	37.50	9.50	7.50	7.00	5.00	4 50	4.00
Plain,	*4200	33.00	8 75	6.75	6.25	4.00	3.75	3.50

* Same shape as No. 4100.   Set with Gilt Cream and Slop, $3.00 extra.

109. Tea set. Meriden Britannia Co., 1861. The International Silver Company Historical Library.

German silver or Britannia, and today it is often difficult to determine whether a base-metal example was once plated. An illustration from the 1861 catalogue of the Meriden Britannia Co. shows a tea set that resembles the gold-plated example discussed earlier (Illus. 109). The engraver made the decoration look like *repoussé* work, which would have been chased, but it also was sold engraved or plain.

The rococo was the style favored for a quantity of small boxes, cups, and trays. Occasionally the decoration was ambitious and the designer would include naturalistic small animals or figures. These rarely were acclaimed. Probably well-taken was the comment of the author of a review of "The Industry of All Nations" (the New York Crystal Palace exhibition of 1853): "We cannot help expressing our regret that skill and labor of any kind should have been wasted on a design of such unequivocal and unmitigated absurdity . . . Three wild cats, turned tail foremost towards the trunk of a tree, and snarling at two others in its branches would be ridiculous wherever perpetrated, but when they are stuck upon the foot of a caster . . ."

Extravagances were generally attempted as innovative variations of the rococo, but as early as the 1850s the Renaissance revival was being introduced. It was considered appropriate for the dining room, yet it was not popular for flatware or tableware. Renaissance revival silver became prominent in the 1860s, although rare examples of a decade earlier may be found. While those made before 1860 may be decorated with ornament in relief, the typical examples of Renaissance revival silver are in designs that are flat. With the exception of stamped profiles resembling medallions which are focal points of many pieces, the decoration is generally engraved and the motifs vary from the almost abstract shell and pediment to elaborate leaf-and-flower garland designs that require more precise work. The style was as important for the relatively simple household as the most elegant.

Renaissance revival design involved using a lot more than the Renaissance as a source of inspiration. The designer chose anything he considered classical as ornament, from ancient Greek to Robert Adam or Empire. Forms were distinctively nineteenth-century inventions to suit the period. Tall narrow shapes were preferred as a reaction to the squat proportion of rococo revival examples.

The Renaissance revival pieces were made to sell at prices ranging from what would seem high today to those that must have been bargains, and the quality of workmanship is often an obvious indication of the original price. However, the cheaper examples may be better designed so the collector would do well to consider esthetics rather than the quality of details. The most handsomely drawn classical motifs may appear on a piece that is ungainly, or schematic machine engraving may be the perfect complement to a piece.

An example of the finest quality workmanship is a vegetable dish made by the Gorham Manufacturing Company as a special order (Illus. 110). George Peabody, an admiring philanthropist, presented the dish to Cyrus W. Field as part of a large silver service which was just one of the many gifts he received when the Atlantic Cable was finally in working order in 1866.

110. Vegetable dish. Gorham Manufacturing Company, 1866. The Museum of the City of New York, gift of Newcomb Carlton.

The profile portrait of Field is visible in the illustration and on the other side is one of the donor, Mr. Peabody, a New Englander whose gifts to the needy and to educational institutions were famous. The flat cover emphasizes the basic angularity characteristic of the Renaissance revival. The lion, the Greek key, and the profile, the leaf-and-wheat border are all classical and in the right spirit. The border is probably where the quality is most obvious. The leaves and the wheat are rendered in perspective and as if they were a part of a fine sculptural still life. As ordinary as the lion finial is since it appears to be the standard model, it was executed with skill.

The trowel used to lay the corner stone of the Tammany Society of New York in 1867 is much less extraordinary (Illus. 111). The maker, Francis W. Cooper, is well known for Gothic revival ecclesiastic silver. Made as a special commemorative piece, the engraving is fine in its restraint and the picture of the Indian is a good repetition of a popular image. There are many other examples of small pieces especially decorated to commemorate an event.

Sets of tableware of the 1860s and later are sometimes much larger than those common today, but fairly simple services for twelve are also found (Illus. 112). Martin S. Smith, a silversmith of Detroit, provided the wedding present for William Hanna and Clara Keith

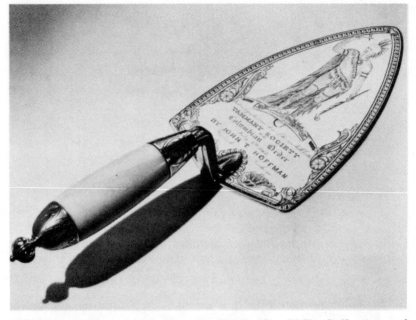

111. Trowel. Francis W. Cooper (1840–68), 1867. Collections of Greenfield Village and the Henry Ford Museum, Dearborn, Michigan.

in 1867. The pattern is elaborate but flat with classical elements more richly applied than would be usual at the time. The leaves and rosettes are elegantly executed as part of a design that must have appeared inventive when new.

On cruets and other pieces for the table, the classical elements suggest the date. Classical busts and eagles are more likely to be found on work before 1880 than after (Illus. 113). The stand by Reed and Barton, patented March 30, 1869, has both Renaissance and medieval motifs. The eagle, the sphinxes, and the scrolls are of much different inspiration than the small warriors in the center. The overall design is more ambitious than that of many sterling pieces.

Silver plate was often as fashionably conceived as sterling. Although economies should be evident in their manufacture, the quality of the design of plate may be at least as high as the sterling. The designs that do not appear successful today are those that have been

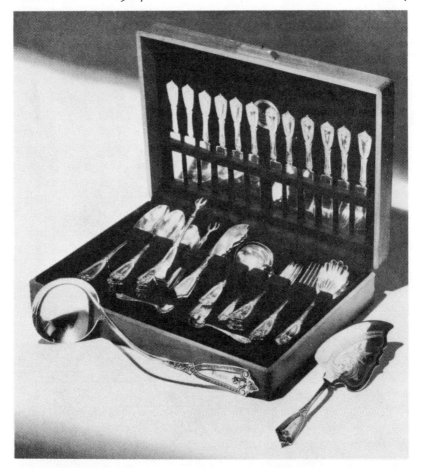

112. 67-piece tableware service. Martin S. Smith, 1867. Collections of Greenfield Village and the Henry Ford Museum, Dearborn, Michigan.

executed badly. On the other hand, success is apparent in the tea set made by the Meriden Britannia Co. in 1867 (Illus. 114). The basic forms were stamped out in volume with the cast legs and profiles applied by a mass technique. Even the engraving was conceived for large-scale production. Method is less important than the total conception of the design. Each detail is part of an integrated scheme that is effective. Whoever was responsible for the results took the

113. Cruet stand. Reed and Barton, patented 1869. The Museum of the City of New York, gift of Dr. Charles Elsberg.

capabilities of the machinery and men into consideration to create good work. In collecting plate products it is possible to turn up pieces in designs that are well conceived, such as this, but then it may take some experience to find the Renaissance revival a suitable substitute for eighteenth-century efforts.

A silver-plated beverage service marked by Martin S. Smith of De-

114. *Tea set, silver plate. Meriden Britannia Co., 1867. The International Silver Company Historical Library.*

115. *Beverage service. Martin S. Smith, 1867. Collections of Greenfield Village and the Henry Ford Museum, Dearborn, Michigan.*

116. Inkstand. Wood and Hughes, 1872. Courtesy of the Museum of the City of New York.

troit and part of the wedding silver of Mr. and Mrs. William Hanna bears a strong resemblance to the Meriden set (Illus. 115). The cast parts are very similar and the forms are alike. Compare the pitchers and the teapots to see how close the two sets can be. The difference in the engraving is a matter of little consequence since the spirit is the same for both sets. Meriden was the country's largest producer and possibly Smith was simply a retail outlet for their plated work.

The mixture of the Renaissance revival motifs with more exotic elements began by the 1870s. An inkwell commissioned as a gift to John T. Hoffman to commemorate his position between 1869–72 as Commander-in-Chief of the National Guard of the State of New York has both classical and Middle Eastern motifs in its design (Illus. 116). Made by Wood and Hughes in about 1872,

117. *Vertically revolving caster set. Meriden Britannia Co., 1860. The International Silver Company Historical Library.*

118. *Toilet set. Meriden Britannia Co., 1867. The International Silver Company Historical Library.*

the center standard is capped by a helmeted classical head and the tray rests on winged and scrolled lion's paw feet. The ink bottle covers are topped by domed covers reminiscent of Islamic forms although they bear fleur-de-lis motifs. The maker, Wood and Hughes, had been prominent in the 1840s and was one of a group of fine silversmiths who continued to operate independently until the end of the nineteenth century.

A revolving caster patented by one Mr. Green in 1860 was manufactured by Meriden Britannia Co. (Illus. 117). Its Renaissance revival motifs have been cast in a base metal plated with silver. Cut-glass bottles were of either English or New England origin. This is just one of countless patented devices made for the table. Silver plate was the metal popular for objects designed for comfort. Toilet stands were made to hold colognes, oils, and powders. They were sometimes made up of a single bottle, but the most elaborate examples were parts of sets that included brushes, combs, and mirrors. A modest example by the Meriden Britannia Co. had a plated stand with classical decoration (Illus. 118). The opaline (or translucent light-colored glass) bottles carry on the classical scheme in form as well as ornament. This was illustrated in an 1867 catalogue of Meriden Britannia.

Renaissance revival designs were important until the end of the decade of the 1870s, but as time went on there was an increased interest in the exotic as well as the more accurate reproduction of eighteenth-century forms. The Renaissance revival was the final style based on a relatively free interpretation of historic models.

CHAPTER VII

Eclectic and Academic Design: 1870–1900

The shift in fashion that began in the 1870s inspired two contrasting approaches to design which can be differentiated as the "academic" and "eclectic." Each relates to a trend that is most obvious in architecture. The academic was dependent upon the careful study of traditional (mainly eighteenth century) design. It resulted in a body of new work based on major styles before 1800 and featured rococo and neo-classical interpretations. Although the objective was adaptation rather than blind imitation, the academic pieces are sometimes close to outright reproductions of the early models. Eclectic design, on the other hand, was characterized by the introduction of new shapes and less familiar ornament. The eclectic designers sought inspiration in a variety of sources although most of their new ideas came from the study of Oriental and Near Eastern art. Eclectic designers were aware of the growing number of reformers who regarded Near and Far Eastern forms as more functional and desirable than the more traditional classical examples.

Although the eclectic approach had its roots in the reform movement, designers rarely followed the suggestions of the English reformers very closely. The reform philosophy was expressed most popularly in Charles Eastlake's good design primer *Hints on Household Taste* which was published first in London in 1868 and then in Boston in 1872. Eastlake believed design generally was at a low ebb,

119. *Coffeepot, creamer, and sugar bowl. Tiffany and Co., 1874. The Museum of the City of New York, loaned by Alfred M. F. Kiddle.*

and in silver particularly there was an over-emphasis on ornament. He suggested simplicity to show off the quality of the metal. He felt "Vessels of silver should be composed of thin plate, and the best means of decorating them is either by piercing the metal with open-work ornament, engraved (i.e., non-naturalistic) patterns, or by *repoussé* decoration, which consists in beating out the silver from inside into bosses and arabesques."

While eclectic designers did not always show the restraint that Eastlake desired, they did avoid the more fanciful floral patterns and miniature figures he abhorred.

Near Eastern ewers were a popular source for eclectic designs of the 1870s. Tiffany and Co. produced a tea service in which this basic design was the point of departure for each of the pieces (Illus. 119). The *repoussé* decoration was adapted from painted tiles with results that were a successful expression of an Eastlake idea. Just about the same design was repeated on a tea set by one of the silver-plate manufacturers with the plated version simplified to reduce the cost of manufacture. Instead of the long floral panels on the Tiffany pieces, the decoration was modified into a small repeating pattern that could be stamped on the metal quickly.

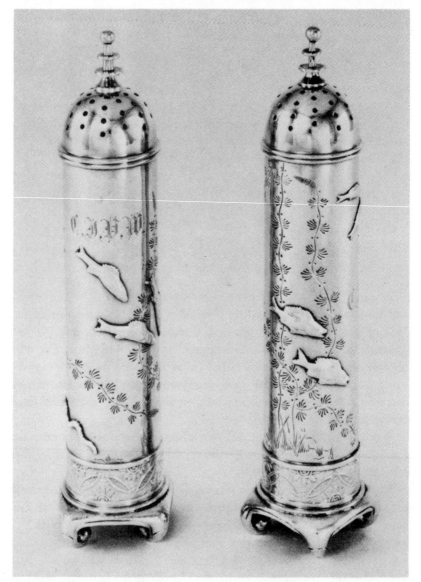

120. *Pepper shakers. Tiffany and Co., 1874. The Museum of the City of New York, bequest of Katharine Van Wyck Haddock.*

Another exotic source of inspiration, Japanese metalwork, is reflected in a number of Tiffany and Co. designs executed between 1870 and 1900. A pair of shakers made of sterling silver has applied decoration in the form of fish and is engraved in a sea-weed pattern on tall narrow cylinders that are in the spirit of Japanese bronze and pottery (Illus. 120). The shakers are particularly important as evidence of the more serious side of Japanese-influenced design. This interest in things Japanese had a more popular manifestation in which designers found the motifs they were to employ in the prints and the decorative papers that were popular Japanese exports. The more serious designers incorporated elements familiar from Japanese metalwork and ceramics that were being imported.

The geographical source was the same but the motifs and the actual inspiration were very different in a silver-plated tea set shown in a catalogue of about 1878 by the Meriden Britannia Company. The Meriden example is less pure (Illus. 121). The unusual shapes are more or less Oriental, but the finials and the relief ornament on the handles and legs are Greco-Roman. A closer look at the center bands will reveal the flat engraved floral pattern includes a variety of petals associated with Japanese porcelain decoration.

The variations in the designs of the plated wares are endless. Japanese elements were mixed with traditional Western motifs in any number of different ways. Shapes are simple and more Oriental than Occidental in their seemingly functional designs. There is a contrast between the cast feet, handles, spouts and finials, and engraved main surfaces on a coffeepot that has been dated 1872 (Illus. 122). It has classical bearded heads as feet and classical leaf ornament in relief above the feet as well as below the spout and handle. The large bird finial is more or less Japanese since it is the kind of bird seen in Japanese prints although it is rendered as realistically as a classical figure.

On a Meriden Britannia Co. hot-water urn a frieze based on a classical Roman mythological theme is combined with the Oriental (Illus. 123). The date January 26, 1869 on the spigot is when a patent was obtained for this device and about nine years before this piece was made. A matte surface was used as a background for

No. 1916. EMBOSSED CHASED TEA SET.

121. Tea set. Meriden Britannia Co., 1878. The International Silver Company Historical Library.

flat linear floral patterns that are as geometric as the flashiest Oriental designs of the period. The lion was a standard motif for finials and it is repeated on a tureen that also bears the band of classical mythological figures (Illus. 124). The engraving on the main part of the body is different. It has a flat floral panel surrounded by more freely executed flowers, again reminiscent of the colorful decorative Japanese papers. The plain covers were stamped out of sheets of metal by the usual mass-production technique.

The silver on plated examples of this type often wears so that a black spot that looks like tarnish may resist being polished away. The top surface on plated ware will in time give way to a dark gray base metal. While careful replating can be very successful, often a piece will become too bright after restoration.

The ice-water or tilting pitcher is still another of the new forms of the late nineteenth century. An example by the Meriden Britannia Co. has been dated 1886 (Illus. 125). Its *repoussé* floral bands were

122. Coffeepot. Webster Manufacturing Co., 1872. The International Silver Company Historical Library.

stamped out in quantity and applied to the piece. The decoration is based on Near Eastern designs. The engraving is more Oriental than Occidental, but the handle and spout are, nonethless, classical.

Each of the pieces of plated silver are restrained but clearly a manifestation of the flamboyance close to universal in the last quarter of the nineteenth century.

Another tea set by Tiffany suggests the more experimental tendencies that represent another facet of design in the 1880s (Illus. 126).

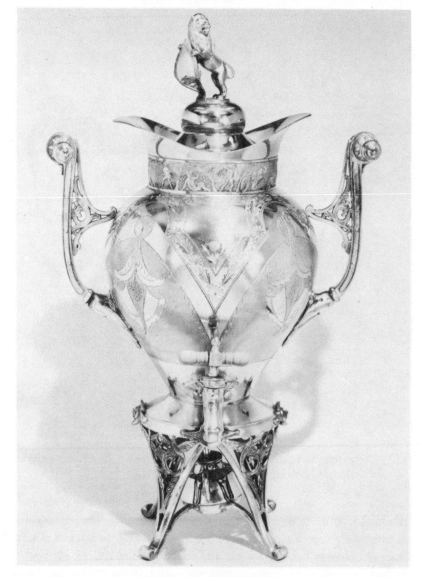

123. Hot-water urn on stand. Meriden Britannia Co., 1878. The International Silver Company Historical Library.

124. Tureen and ladle. Meriden Britannia Co., 1878. The International Silver Company Historical Library.

The dark areas on the pot are a reddish enamel. The designer adapted a Near Eastern form which he enlivened by introducing color. Eastlake had alluded to the advantages of enamel decoration and the designer may well have followed his suggestion. The richness is more subtle yet more impressive in this than in the plated examples. Colored enamels had been an important phase of goldsmiths' work in the sixteenth century, but revivals of the technique of enameling in the nineteenth century are relatively rare. It was a costly process that took more than average skills and one that was not easily applied to mass production. Virtuoso efforts by goldsmiths on the Continent had included the use of enamel in Renaissance revival jewelry.

125. Ice pitcher (or tilting pitcher). Meriden Britannia Co., 1886. The International Silver Company Historical Library.

The most famous exotic efforts that were based on the use of exotic design sources are the Pan-Slavic enamels that were a familiar Russian product in the 1870s. While there is slight possibility of any direct connection, the use of enamel was not unique and was a logical way of pointing up the fact that a piece was the work of an individual craftsman.

More characteristic of the period are the many efforts to suggest opulence in simply made mass-produced work. These are examples that often follow the academic approach in designs that Eastlake would have disliked. A spoon holder with cast silver-plated frame holding a pressed glass bowl in the popular tree-of-life pattern is representative of typical work of the time (Illus. 127). The rustic branch design is basically a whimsical rococo revival design. It was inexpensively made, however, and an example of the fashionable academic and conservative work available on the popular market.

In the late 1870s, the art glass that was beginning to achieve pop-

126. Teapot. Tiffany and Co., 1888. The Metropolitan Museum of Art, gift of a friend of the Museum, 1897.

ularity as opulent decoration for middle-class interiors was also used on silver-plated frames. Art glass was brightly colored and exotically shaped to look difficult to make and to answer the demand for impressive, unusual pieces. The silver-plate manufacturers obtained the glass inserts from both American and English glass manufacturers. More than one advertisement describes the glass as Bristol to suggest its English origin, although it would have been possible to obtain similar pieces from American sources. A bowl and stand made by the Meriden Britannia Co. about 1880 has flat, classical floral dec-

127. Spoon holder with glass liner. Meriden Britannia Co., 1879 (glass by Portland Glass Co.). The International Silver Company Historical Library.

128. Glass bowl with silver stand. Meriden Britannia Co., about 1880. The International Silver Company Historical Library.

oration on its feet and an angel inspired by Roman art on disks at the sides of the handles (Illus. 128).

The Victorian home was more than amply furnished with small objects. One form—the tray in the entrance hall on which calling cards were left—was made in both academic and eclectic design. One more or less typical example was made in the Japanese spirit by the Meriden Silver Plate Co. in about 1885 (Illus. 129). The cast birds and flowers are just a little blurred in a complex design that consists of a wide variety of motifs. Often the manufacturers were too ambitious and they could not avoid imperfections in the details. Some connoisseurs find the lack of crispness an asset since it reduces the glitter. This form was called a card receiver in contemporary sales catalogues.

Silver-plate manufacturers produced a number of small decorative items that were more decorative than functional. One example is the jewel box, or "Jewel Casket" as it was called in catalogues of the 1870s. It was what every household required for the storage of small pins and the like. Several patents were issued to protect the ingenious devices invented to ease opening and closing these containers (Illus. 130). The designs reflect the popularity of the Oriental. The group illustrated were made over a twenty-year period, but differences between them are due to the broad range of styles that was available

129. Card receiver. Meriden Silver Plate Co., about 1885. The International Silver Company Historical Library.

rather than changes that evolved. The silver-plate manufacturers were interested in pleasing every taste so they offered all possible variety. The flat patterns of the two examples on the right were inspired by the fad for Japanese design. Both were made first in the 1870s. Designs for the two on the left are not as easily traced. The cylindrical box has flowers that are classical, but the form must have been a new invention. The round box, below, is decorated with a repeating double scroll and rosette that might have been inspired by the Ancient Egyptian art which was very popular in the 1870s because publications about it were coming out.

Other jewel caskets had glass boxes in silver frames, such as one by the Derby Silver Co. of Derby, Connecticut (Illus. 131). The pink-glass box adorned with delicate floral motifs echoes the eighteenth century while the flowers on the frame are flattened in a manner reminiscent of floral designs in Japanese pictures.

Since sales rather than strong esthetic convictions were the main motivating factor in the design of most mass-produced silver in the

130. *Jewel caskets.* TOP LEFT: *Wilcox Silver Plate Co., about 1896.*
TOP RIGHT: *Meriden Britannia Co., 1879.* BOTTOM LEFT: *Meriden Britannia Co., 1879.* BOTTOM RIGHT: *Meriden Britannia Co., 1873–77.*
The International Silver Company Historical Library.

131. Glass box in silver frame. Derby Silver Co., 1883. The International Silver Company Historical Library.

last quarter of the nineteenth century, there is a broad variety. The jewel caskets reflect the varying tastes of a public interested in the revivalism that expoited continual references to eighteenth-century models as well as more revolutionary efforts that were based on the study of the exotic—Oriental or Near Eastern. The boxes were low-priced luxuries that also prove how fashion had become universal in the late nineteenth century. It was not simply the more opulent houses but those of the middle classes that could boast the latest designs. Both types of houses were either furnished with objects that were up-to-the-minute or those that were selected by conservatives who preferred designs that were decades old.

The shift in taste towards the end of the century is made particularly clear in a selection of four small boxes that appear in a single photograph (Illus. 132). The rectangular box in the lower left corner is decorated with the meander or Greek-key pattern in a flat design typical of the 1870s. In the upper right-hand corner is a box ornamented with high-relief swirls and a winged angel that appears to be an interpretation of the Art Nouveau style cleaned up for middle-class acceptance. In French and German silver the figure is a

132. *Jewel caskets.* TOP LEFT: *Derby Silver Co., about 1896.* TOP RIGHT: *Derby Silver Co., (Victor Silver Co.), early 1900s.* BOTTOM LEFT: *Middletown Plate Co., about 1874.* BOTTOM RIGHT: *Wilcox Silver Plate Co., about 1896. The International Silver Company Historical Library.*

woman with long hair who looks seductive and as though she had nothing on under the hair which covers her body. Here, the angel is sufficiently innocent and safe to avoid shocking any potential customer. The flowing lines of the box are an aspect of the design that characterizes a number of the more ambitious but inexpensive pieces of the early 1900s. These are all stamped out in quantity to simulate the hand-hammered *repoussé* ornament. The simplicity of the Art Nouveau patterns was an ideal vehicle for the technique. The other boxes are embellished with relief ornament that has been cast and applied. The eighteenth-century rococo was the source of inspiration for designs that are typical of late nineteenth-century efforts.

Silver manufacturers at the end of the nineteenth century were producing an extensive line of decorative objects for the home. Having succeeded in the dining room, they advanced through the house offering bedroom, parlor, library, and dressing-room accessories. They also made cases and flasks for the pocket. Major manufacturers published catalogues that show the variety of wares in what was predominantly a rococo revival style. The popularity of *repoussé* ornament is evident on both silver and silver plate.

The collector may find the search for one or more of the small forms rewarding. Small flat match cases (which sometimes are mistaken for card cases) were made in the various styles of the period and a group of ten will illustrate the types of ornament popular at the turn of the century.

Flasks are another form that were very decorative at the turn of the century. The silver companies offered some flasks in brilliant-cut glass that would shred pockets if not enclosed in some kind of protective bag, but most were all metal. Overall floral designs were popular along with designs consisting of a single figure, a baseball player or an Indian, for example.

Dresser sets that came into popularity first in the 1870s consisted of trays and several cosmetic jars as well as brushes and mirrors. In the 1880s it was possible to buy a small cylindrical box the shape of an oversized lipstick that was made to store hairpins, and a device resembling a scissors with dull round ends that was a glove stretcher. Both were made to match other items put on the dresser top. While *repoussé* ornament was the most popular, there were designs in flat patterns as well.

By the end of the century, the dining room table was embellished with objects that were as significant for their amusement value as their esthetic qualities. Cute little figures pulling carts or holding containers of one kind or another were introduced to add some zest to the more ordinary tablewares. These novelties were the nineteenth-century version of the more impressive figures that goldsmiths had made in the sixteenth and seventeenth centuries, but they are cute rather than impressive. The figures appear on salts, compotes, and other containers as well, but napkin rings are a particularly popular vehicle for these ideal examples of the Victorian approach. Sentimental, pretentious, but amusing, the figures were designed to appeal broadly. The figural rings hold napkins but also have a place for pepper, salt, and sometimes vinegar. Little cupids are part of two

133. Casters with napkin rings. LEFT: *Wilcox Silver Plate Co., about 1873.* CENTER: *Meriden Britannia Co., 1873.* RIGHT: *Simpson, Hall, Miller & Co., 1879. The International Silver Company Historical Library.*

illustrated, while the other has floral decoration exclusively (Illus. 133). The figures are not great examples of sculpture, but they add to the liveliness of the pieces. These were first made in the 1870s. Even simple rings without places for condiments were made with figures as anchors to keep the standing ring stationary. One Meriden Britannia Co. napkin ring of the 1880s had a Kate Greenaway girl serving as the anchor (Illus. 134). Kate Greenaway was the English water-colorist whose children's book illustrations had captivated two continents from the 1870s until her death in 1901. In the books, Greenaway children were dressed in a curious style which was a revival of early nineteenth-century clothing. The quaint outfits were copied by sewing mothers as well as clothing manufacturers everywhere. This girl with a muff is dressed in clothing in the Greenaway spirit. Another subject popular for the holders was a variety of animals. Generally sentimental, the quality of the figures rendered varied. While these forms are clearly nineteenth-century inventions, occasionally they were based on eighteenth-century models of some

134. Napkin ring. Meriden Britannia Co., 1886. The International Silver Company Historical Library.

kind. The small porcelain animals and figures as well as bottles or tureens in the shape of animals that are well-known eighteenth-century forms were an inspiration to nineteenth-century designers. The major difference between the work of the two centuries is in the relationship between the decorative animals and more ambitious art. The eighteenth-century porcelain figures were conceived in much the same way as any major work of art while the nineteenth-century silver examples are more closely related to popular illustrations of their day. This small silver sculpture is stylized to have immediate appeal, and its quality is in its success as popular art. Animals or people, their merit is in how easily they arouse an emotional response.

A silver salt shaker of about 1880 that was sold at Tiffany and Co. is an illustration of the popular approach in any object that was originally expensive (Illus. 135). The monkey turned out to be very nearly human and a caricature. It is close to eighteenth-century renditions of the subject, but there is a distinctively nineteenth-century touch in the contrast between the stylized facial features and the more convincingly detailed fur.

Stylization was emphasized as a means of cheapening production

135. *Salt shaker. Tiffany and Co.,
about 1880. The Museum of the
City of New York, gift of Miss
Susan Dwight Bliss.*

costs for countless small decorative objects. The results are often
successful since the omissions required to simplify the mold might
enable the designer to capture the essence of a subject in a figure
that was essentially representative of the popular taste of its period.
In the group of knife rests by the Meriden Britannia Co., the small
sculptural elements are simple yet detailed since nineteenth-century
artists could not resist all possible embellishments (Illus. 136).

Silver plate was the metal preferred for a number of special forms
that were used on the table. Butter dishes, for example, were
possibly subject to more wear than many people thought good for
silver. Whatever the reason, the plated silver examples are better
known. The three examples illustrated reflect the main design trends
of the time (Illus. 137). The dishes on the right and left follow
the academic approach. Simpson, Hall, Miller and Company, manufacturers of the dish to the right have made a piece of great restraint
that is essentially traditional. The cow finial was borrowed from
ceramic examples of the eighteenth century and while the overall

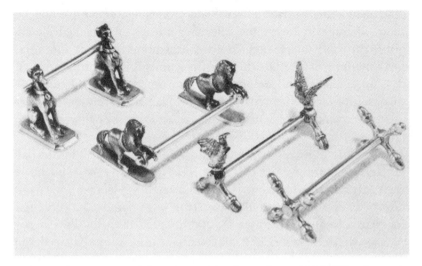

136. *Knife rests. Meriden Britannia Co., about 1886. The International Silver Company Historical Library.*

shape is curiously typical of the 1880s, with the exception of the feet the rest of the design is also related to eighteenth-century work. The Meriden Britannia Co. butter dish of 1896, on the left, is not like eighteenth-century butter dishes, but the wide fluting that covers the entire piece was inspired by eighteenth-century design. On the

137. *Butter dishes.* LFET: *Meriden Britannia Co., 1896.* CENTER: *Wilcox Silver Plate Co., 1884.* RIGHT: *Simpson, Hall, Miller & Co., about 1886. The International Silver Company Historical Library.*

other hand, the Wilcox Silver Plate Company responsible for the center example followed the eclectic approach in ornamenting the dish with bands of Japanese-inspired decoration. Each of the dishes is a variation of the late nineteenth-century butter dish form. All have inner liners and are practical functional pieces. Occasionally silversmiths made the older form, the miniature butter tub that was more common in porcelain or earthenware, but those are very rare.

Compiling a list of all the unusual forms produced in the late nineteenth century is very difficult. Silver and silver-plate manufacturers attempted to make anything that might be left out on a table, dresser, or stand of any kind. Some items were popular and produced for years; others were not salable and dropped from the line shortly. Among the more surprising nineteenth-century pieces is a cocktail

138. Cocktail shaker. Unidentified maker. Patented 1885. Courtesy of the Museum of the City of New York.

139. Lavatory set. Meriden Britannia Co., 1890. The International Silver Company Historical Library.

shaker patented in 1885 (Illus. 138). So far the actual patent has not been found because while the date is clear, the name is obliterated and no patent for a cocktail shaker is listed for 1885. Possibly the patent is for the plated silver metal. The beaded border and the general detailing make the early date logical although at first glance the shaker appears to be of 1920 vintage.

Silver and plated silver lavatory sets were a popular luxury of the turn of the century. These provided containers and utensils for washing and preparing for dressing—the soap, water, cologne, hair oil, and powders used in getting ready to face the world. The ceramic versions were more practical but not as ostentatious. The decoration, engraved and stamped out in *repoussé* patterns, generally follows traditional models. The rococo seen on a Meriden Britannia Co. set is typical (Illus. 139). While whole sets are rare, boxes or bottles may be found more readily. The run-of-the-mill piece is of fairly

140. Punch bowl. Gorham Manufacturing Co., 1905. The Museum of the City of New York, gift of Frederick Sheffield.

poor quality, but every company put effort into producing some well-made sets. Engraving should be examined with care to be sure of a finely made example.

Punch bowls were the silver manufacturer's delight since the form was a popular presentation piece. Many were made of the finest sterling to memorialize an event or to be offered as a token of thanks. The bowl given to William Williams by the employees of Ellis Island in 1905 was a superior effort of the Gorham Silver Company (Illus. 140). Made at the time they were producing the "Martelé" line that was inspired by the Arts and Crafts Movement, the Williams bowl is classical and reminiscent of designs fashionable in the 1820s. It is an example that shows that the knowledge of traditional techniques was not lost in the nineteenth century. Proportions differ from those of earlier models and the ornament is more detailed. The leaves on Mr. Williams' bowl have many more veins than those of the 1820s.

Samuel Kirk and Son were also busily at work making presentation pieces at the turn of the century. Having developed a technique for

141. Punch bowl. Samuel Kirk & Son, Inc., about 1901. The Maryland Historical Society, on loan from Samuel Kirk & Son, Inc.

elegant *repoussé* work, the Kirk presentation pieces often have unusual relief scenes. One punch bowl has Bowling Brook Stud Farm of Carroll County, Maryland, represented (Illus. 141). More ordinary examples are restricted to elaborate floral designs in the same kind of relief designs. The Kirk approach was used by a few competitors, but it is distinctive.

Elegant but less expensive were the punch bowls by Meriden Britannia (Illus. 142). Glass and plated silver were often used in combination for economy as much as for the practicality of having an easily removable liner to fill. Grapes were the logical ornamental detail frequently used with the gamut of rococo scroll-and-leaf motifs.

The basic concepts of traditional design followed in 1900 remained working principles into the 1930s. Essentially, forms were determined by contemporary needs and familiar ornament from earlier styles was applied to these forms. The holloware shapes were

142. Punch set. Meriden Britannia Co., about 1896. The International Silver Company Historical Library.

stamped out and bands of *repoussé* added in rococo or neo-classical patterns. Proportions were varied as tastes changed from decade to decade. The eclectic or more adventuresome design gradually lost out to other radical tendencies that had begun to have influence at the end of the century.

CHAPTER VIII

Twentieth-Century Possibilities

The break between the nineteenth and twentieth centuries is not as sharp and clean in the history of American silver as it might be. The adventuresome designers had made their first inroads in the nineteenth century and in many cases simply continued what they had begun before 1900. For example, the shift from using the exotic Japanese models to devising a new vocabulary of ornament had begun in the graphic arts as early as the 1880s but is best known in American silver at the beginning of the twentieth century.

Also, the traditional revivalist approach to design changed more in appearance than philosophy shortly after 1900. The silver of the 1880s and 1890s is generally heavier in proportion than that of the twentieth century, although traditional designs both before and after 1900 are based on a careful study and faithful repetition of eighteenth-century models.

Collectors who specialize in twentieth-century objects generally concentrate on work in the more revolutionary designs. They prefer Art Moderne, Art Nouveau, and Art Deco to the objects in the revival styles that have comprised the greater part of the silver output since 1900. The collector who wants to find bargains would do well to investigate the neglected work of the traditionalist silver designers of the 1900–30 period to ferret out the better examples. It will take patience and a keen eye because much of the revival work is not very good. The objective of too many manufacturers was to create work as elaborate as possible for instant appeal. They ignored the challenges of making their silver well, lasting, and functional. A great part of their output was designed without considering the techniques employed so that details were not executed well. When ornament is stamped rather than engraved, the details have to be modified—and too often this was not done.

Since eighteenth-century forms were raised, and those of the twentieth century are stamped out, it takes some modification of shapes to follow early models, but this has often been taken into consideration. Traditional designs conceived with an understanding of the restrictions of mass-production techniques are worth acquiring. Although the first efforts date from the 1880s, the twentieth century has witnessed the major aspects of the crafts revival. A number of silversmiths working in close to eighteenth-century techniques have been active making silver in relatively new designs. While their production has been small in comparison to the enormous output of the large manufacturers, it is significant. The first of these men and women were participants in the Arts and Crafts Movement. They followed the philosophy of William Morris. This philosophy resulted in designs that are simple and functional. The craftmen showed their admiration for the basic sheen and texture of silver by devising shapes that show it off best. Proud of the fact they used old techniques, they often omitted the final steps of burnishing and polishing in order to leave the hammer marks applied during the raising of a piece. While they have tended to work in adventuresome styles, some found inspiration in the simpler forms of eighteenth-century origin. Bowls and pitchers echoing Paul Revere and other colonial American craftsmen were popular products of silversmiths who revived the craft tradition.

The collector interested in the work of this century should not be concerned with whether a piece was handmade or mass-produced. The most crucial question is how successfully it was designed. In 1937, when Art Moderne was at its height, the Metropolitan Museum organized a contemporary silver exhibition to show the best of what was being made. Richard Bache, the curator who organized the exhibition, included mass-produced and hand-crafted objects in the same competition for prizes because he discovered design was more basic than technique.

Large producers had been forced into being more conservative in design because it was a way of assuring mass appeal. The high cost of tooling up—making the molds and other special parts—to produce a design, made it essential that each design be produced in quantity. Nonetheless, there were occasional experiments with the novel.

At the beginning of this century, the Art Nouveau was the adventuresome style that attracted designers seeking the novel. It was based on the development of new vocabularies of ornament. One essential characteristic was a sinuous line that was flat or rendered in relief. It could be a plant stem, floral motifs that were elongated and thin, or females represented with long, flowing hair to fit into the typical Art Nouveau vocabulary of ornament. Americans tended to create the Art Nouveau patterns in relief.

Art Nouveau silver made in the United States is relatively rare, but catalogues of the 1900s include many illustrations that prove it was produced. The range of forms was extensive. For example, dresser sets were a popular American Art Nouveau item. The mirrors, combs and brushes and the appropriate containers to be set on a dresser were made of sheets of silver plate stamped in the characteristic relief patterns. They were made by a number of the Connecticut manufacturers such as the Derby Silver Company. Flowers and female heads are two of the most common motifs on dresser sets (Illus. 143). Since the Art Nouveau did not become popular in furniture, glass, or ceramics, it is surprising to see how Americans kept up with the latest fashion in silver.

The "Confection Epergne" that appeared in catalogues of The Victor Silver Co., a division of the Derby Silver Company, is distinctively Art Nouveau (Illus. 144). The characteristic sinuous line was used as a support rather than a border on the stand for the bowls. The center figure is more demure and middle class than those on European examples, but she is as thin as any of the more sirenlike European figures. The silver-plated versions of the style that were at once fashionable and inoffensive are often subdued examples of the Art Nouveau.

A lot more study is needed to learn more about the finer silver

143. *Brush from dresser set. Derby Silver Co. (?), 1905. Courtesy of the Brooklyn Museum, Lever Fund, 1967.*

144. *Confection epergne. Derby Silver Co. (Victor Silver Co.), 1900–10. The International Silver Company Historical Library.*

makers. Firms like that of Tiffany and Company, which manufactured silver expensively, were able to produce elaborate wares in designs of more limited appeal. Since production was small, very little is known of these early twentieth-century efforts. It will not be possible to discuss the significance of each style until more is known about this phase of silver production. At this point a few manufacturers have been singled out by collectors.

Unger is the name of one of the manufacturing companies of the turn-of-the-century that has attracted attention because of its Art Nouveau production. Working in sterling silver, the Unger Brothers' catalogue listed flatware, holloware, dresser sets, and jewelry. Richly ornate, handsomely detailed work was characteristic of their output. A group of small objects in the Metropolitan Museum suggests

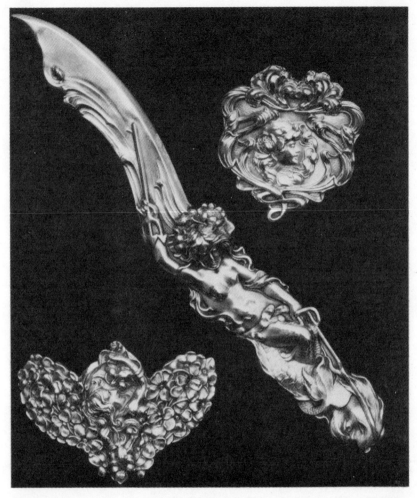

145. Letter opener, brooch, belt buckle. Unger Brothers, 1905. The Metropolitan Museum of Art, gift of Ron Kane, 1967.

the quality of typical efforts (Illus. 145). Flowers and hair are mixed in compositions typical of the Art Nouveau. The letter opener has as its main decoration a determined mermaid holding a triton. Her dour facial expression brings Aubrey Beardsley to mind because it seems to have been inspired by the peculiarly psychotic imagery familiar in that turn-of-the-century English artist's work.

One of the larger silver manufacturers, the Gorham Company, offered a line of silver objects in a variation of the Art Nouveau style which they called "Martelé." The name is French for hammered, and the objects have surfaces given texture by being hit with hammers. This is an effect that was favored by craftsmen allied to the Arts and Crafts Movement. The ornament on these pieces consisted of flowers and borders of leaves in the Art Nouveau spirit. The line included a variety of forms, from punch bowl to dresser set. It was Gorham's bid for the market of buyers willing to pay extra for finely designed and handsomely made objects. The company employed the services of a designer named William C. Codman to develop the "Martelé" as well as other lines in the more adventuresome fashions of the day. He had trained in England and some of his innovations were related to English developments.

Besides the flowery Art Nouveau, there was another direction for the style that involved the use of straight lines in almost geometric patterns. The inspiration for this kind of design was in early Celtic and Viking art. Sometimes these patterns of straight lines were sparked up with additions of enamel in bright colors. Codman had introduced objects reflecting this tendency at Gorham, but so far little is known about the extent of production. They relate to English efforts of the period associated with Liberty and Company.

At the beginning of the century active American participation in the Arts and Crafts Movement is evident in silver. Other crafts had benefited from the founding of the first arts and crafts societies in the 1890s, but there was little work in silver until after 1900. The small group of silversmiths working as artist-craftsmen is just being rediscovered. Their self-consciousness is revealed in their insistence on proving their work was handmade. They preferred the uneven hammered surfaces that were discussed as characteristic of "Martelé." Basically, designs of arts and crafts silver in the first decade of this century often were inspired by the geometric aspect of the Art Nouveau. Besides the Celtic or pre-Christian Northern European, there was American Indian influence to a minor degree. With the craftsmen intent on fine craftsmanship, when all else failed and no remote source could be used for inspiration, eighteenth-century shapes were models for bowls, pitchers, and trays.

Silversmiths working in traditional techniques have been the real revolutionaries of twentieth-century design. Whether artist-craftsmen following the philosophy of William Morris, or just plain silversmiths, they have been able to experiment and to work on new vocabularies of ornament. Their changes did not entail any kind of lasting expenditures. The factories, on the other hand, used molds and stamping equipment that would be very costly if a specific model could not be produced in the thousands from one tooling set-up. Between 1910 and 1920 the most significant new silver was produced in small quantities by relatively small shops. The craftsmen were carrying on the tradition of the Arts and Crafts Movement while transforming the light forms echoing the Art Nouveau to examples in heavier proportions. While eighteenth-century models were inspiration for some, others were more experimental.

It is difficult to learn about this group of all but forgotten craftsmen. Only a few were represented in the 1972 exhibition, *The Arts and Crafts Movement in America 1876–1916* organized by the Art Museum of Princeton University and the Art Institute of Chicago. The Jarvie Shop and the Kalo Shops in the Chicago area were both included in the exhibition but comparable craftsmen must have been working in Cincinnati, Boston, Cleveland, and Detroit since the Arts and Crafts Movement was strong there also. It will take some hunting to uncover work from these centers. Collectors interested in twentieth-century design should keep the artist-craftsman in mind. They were often the more adventuresome and always the more careful makers.

The First World War slowed down the changes in design between 1914 and 1919 by destroying communications between artists. A careful inspection of work of the period would reveal that a shift was discernible by 1915, as heavier forms replaced the typical elongated objects in the Art Nouveau style. The innovations were occasional, however, until after 1920 when the new style was obvious enough to be identified. Squat proportions, shiny surfaces, and ornament that is at times new and at other times a simplification of eighteenth-century decoration are characteristic of the new style. Its name, Art Deco, was a popular descriptive term that was a corruption of the formal name of the exhibition which gave the style official status, the

"Exposition des arts décoratifs et industriels modernes" of 1925. The style was international although some of its finest products were made in France. Art Deco is an essentially decorative style that offered no startling innovations. Contemporary with the more novel experiments of the German designers associated with The Bauhaus, the Art Deco offered stylized up-dated ornament on forms that were traditional. Its best efforts were very finely made, its finest designs captured the spirit of the moment when synthetic cubism and expressionism were the key styles in painting and sculpture. Americans were as quick to work in this new style of the 1920s as their colleagues in Europe and their contribution was as original.

The style had a fairly wide range. At one extreme, traditional eighteenth-century forms were modified—up-dated—by a general slickening of ornament. At the other extreme, the forms were rendered as basic cubes, globes, and cylinders to look machine-made. These forms were embellished with equally simple decorative elements. The 1920–30 period tended to include more traditionalism, while after 1930 there was an increased use of new-looking forms. The more innovatory approach was also influenced by an awareness of primitive art on the part of many designers. African and pre-Columbian American art influenced some Art Deco design. Many connoisseurs differentiate the decorative art of the 1920s from that of the 1930s and call the former Art Deco and the latter Art Moderne. The justification for the differentiation is in the change of emphasis discernible from fine craftsmanship to novel design.

Innovations include angular forms that appear to have been influenced by the conception of the Synthetic Cubists—that group of painters and sculptors who sought to record space in a new way. Juan Gris, Picasso, and Braque had made a revolutionary statement that was only superficially related to the designers of silver, but the connection is apparent nonetheless. In a way, they might seem closer to Buck Rogers.

Ken Rogers and Lauritz Eichner are two American designers who attracted attention in the 1920s and 1930s for fine work that was produced in limited quantity. Large companies such as Wilcox Silver Plate, Reed and Barton, and Rogers, Lunt and Bowlen also made objects in modern designs.

Twentieth-century design offers challenges that many collectors will prefer to avoid. While fakes are no problem, selecting work that is both well conceived and executed is difficult.

CHAPTER IX

Identifying American Silver

Ideally, the work of an American craftsman or manufacturer should be recognizable in the design of a piece. The American example is simpler than the Old World versions of the same form, American designs are more functional, and the ornament is less intricate. Most collectors would say they can recognize what is American by examining a piece, but few have the confidence it would take to ignore the mark or signature on a piece. All admit it is important to be able to identify marks. There are a number of books that include drawings or photographs of marks used by Americans to simplify identification. The serious student is never satisfied with anything short of comparing actual marks, and he will make an appointment with a curator of a museum collection to see an actual mark or a good photographic close-up with his own piece in hand.

From the seventeenth century to the middle of the nineteenth, American silversmiths applied their signatures to silver by using stamps—metal punches that bore a personal monogram, with a symbol or not, or a full surname. Many pieces of quality were never marked. The American practice differed from the English because in England the finished piece of silver was assayed and if approved would be stamped with three marks in addition to the maker's. The only American silver assay office was in Baltimore from 1814 to 1830, but assay marks are encountered on a range of American examples from the late eighteenth to the mid-nineteenth century. Although the extra marks on New York silver are generally regarded as pseudo hallmarks, it is possible that they were applied after some regulatory checking. At any rate, silver made between about 1780 and 1850 with extra marks may be American.

The work of some men has been valued more highly than comparable efforts by their contemporaries. Paul Revere and Myer Myers, for example, are two whose work brings the highest prices. Both were extremely able but each was matched in quality by competitors who are not as colorful to twentieth-century minds. Revere will be remembered always as the patriot whose daring midnight ride is memorialized by the Longfellow poem. Myers was Jewish and one of few American Jewish silversmiths on record, so that his work is of particular interest to his co-religionists who are twentieth-century collectors. To ease problems of supply, fake marks have been made to apply to unmarked silver that might reasonably be attributed to Revere or Myers. Also the MM of Myers and the PR of Revere were like any number of English PR's and MM's and occasionally the English hallmarks have been removed to make a piece appear to be by one of these more costly makers. There have been fake marks made by casting from marked pieces. While it is troublesome to detect these fake marks on authentic pieces of silver, anyone cautious will become aware of inconsistencies that are most easily explained as fakery.

The practice of using stamps with the letters in relief was all but replaced in the course of the nineteenth century by a process of applying intaglio names and trademarks. These names are printed in letters that frequently look their age. With a little experience and some knowledge of nineteenth-century looks you can begin to distinguish names of the 1830s from those of the 1870s. Patent dates and sometimes patent numbers were also provided on some pieces.

To begin on a job of identifying a piece of silver, looking for the name of the maker on the list that follows may be helpful. Finding it might suggest the next step, but if the name is not on the list and the approximate date of the piece is obvious, consult the bibliography for further study.

The list has dates that are often approximate. Dates in parentheses are the birth and death dates of individuals; the others are dates of activity.

Prominent American Silversmiths and Manufacturers

Ackley, Francis M.	New York, N.Y.	1797–1800
Adams & Shaw Co.	Providence, R.I.	1874–76
	New York, N.Y.	1876–77
	Newark, N.J.	1878–80
Adams, William	New York, N.Y.	1831–42
Adelphi Silver Plate Co.	New York, N.Y.	1890–1904
Akerly & Co.	New York, N.Y.	1850
Allen, Alexander	Rochester, N.Y.	1850
Alvin Corporation	Providence, R.I.	1886–present
Alvin Mfg. Co.		1886–1915
Alvin Silver Co.		1915–20
Purchased by Gorham Corp.		1928
Ames Mfg. Co.	Chicopee, Mass.	1829–1920
Andras & Richard William Andras and Samuel Richard	New York, N.Y.	1797–99
Armstrong, Thomas S.	Brooklyn, N.Y.	1838–40
Aurora Silver Plate Co. (Succeeded by Mulholland Bros.)	Aurora, Ill.	1869–1915

Bachman, Joseph	New York, N.Y.	1855
Bailey & Bros.	Utica, N.Y.	1846–52
Thomas Bailey		
Bailey, Banks & Biddle	Philadelphia, Pa.	1904–present
Co.		
Joseph T. Bailey		1833–39
Bailey & Kitchen		1839–46
Bailey & Co.		1840–?70
Baldwin & Smith	New York, N.Y.	1850–53
Samuel Baldwin		
Richard Smith		
Baldwin & Co.	New York, N.Y.	1840–69
Baldwin, Samuel	New York, N.Y.	1835–60
Downing & Baldwin		1835–60
Baldwin & Smith		1850–53
Baldwin, Stanley	New York, N.Y.	1827–37
S. S. Baldwin & Son		
Ball, Tompkins &	New York, N.Y.	1839–51
Black		
Ball, Black & Co.		1851–76
Bancker, Adrian	New York, N.Y.	1766
Barbour Silver Co.	Hartford, Conn.	1892–98
Became part of In-		
ternational Silver Co.		1898
Bayley, Simeon	New York, N.Y.	1785–97
Van Voorhis, Bayley,		
Coley & Cox		
Bayley & Douglass		1797
Benedict, Andrew	New York, N.Y.	1833–39
A. C. Benedict & Co.		
Benedict, Martin	New York, N.Y.	1825–40
Benedict Mfg. Co.	East Syracuse, N.Y.	1894–1953
Benedict & Scudder	New York, N.Y.	1827–37
Martin Benedict		
Egbert Scudder		
Benedict & Son	New York, N.Y.	1840

Benedict & Squire
  Martin Benedict
  Bela S. Squire Jr.
	New York, N.Y.	1839

Black, Starr & Frost	New York, N.Y.	1876–?1930 1962–present
Boelen, Hendrick (Henricus I)	New York, N.Y.	(1661–91)
Boelen, Hendrick (Henricus II)	New York, N.Y.	(1684–1775)
Boelen, Jacob	New York, N.Y.	(1659–1730)
Boelen, Jacob II	New York, N.Y.	1733–86
Boelen, Jacob III	New York, N.Y.	1785
Brasher, Ephraim	New York, N.Y.	(1744–1810)
Breed, William	Boston, Mass.	1740–61
Caldwell, J. E. & Co.	Philadelphia, Pa.	1839
Casey, Samuel	South Kingston, R.I.	1720–80

Charters, Cann &
  Dunn
  James Charters
  John Cann
  David Dunn
	New York, N.Y.	1850

Churchill & Treadwell	Boston, Mass.	1740–61
Cleveland, Benjamin	Newark, N.J.	1790–1835
Coen, Daniel Bloom	New York, N.Y.	1787–1805
Cowell, William	Boston, Mass.	1682–1736
Cowell, William, Jr.	Boston, Mass.	1713–61
Davis & Galt	Philadelphia, Pa.	1888–1922

Derby Silver Co.
  Became part of In-
  ternational Silver
	Derby and Shelton, Conn.	1873–98
		
		1898

Dominick & Hoff
  Purchased by Reed
  & Barton
	Newark, N.J.
	New York, N.Y.
		1821–1928
		
		1928

Doolittle, Amos	New Haven, Conn.	1754–1832

Dorrance, Samuel	Providence, R.I.	1778-1815
Dummer, Jeremiah	Boston, Mass.	1645-1778
Dunbar, Rufus Davenport	Worcester, Mass.	1807-69
Durgin, Wm. B. & Co.	Concord, N.H.	1853-1931
Purchased by		1905
Gorham Corp.	Providence, R.I.	1931-present
Eastman, Seth	Concord, N.H.	1801-85
Edwards, John	Boston, Mass.	1671-1746
Edwards, Joseph, Jr.	Boston, Mass.	1737-83
Embree, Effingham	New York, N.Y.	1785-91
Eoff, Garrett	New York, N.Y.	1807-45
Eoff & Connor	New York, N.Y.	1834-35
Garrett Eoff		
John H. Connor		
Eoff & Howell	New York, N.Y.	1806-08
Garrett Eoff		
Paul Howell		
Eoff & Moore	New York, N.Y.	1835-40
Eoff & Phyfe	New York, N.Y.	1840-48
Edgar Eoff		
William Phyfe		
Eoff & Shepherd	New York, N.Y.	1824-38
Evans, Henry	New York, N.Y.	1820-35
	Newark, N.J.	1835-63
Evans, Robert	Boston, Mass.	1768-1812
Fairchild & Co.	New York, N.Y.	1837-1922
Founded as Randall & Fairchild		1837-43
Fairchild, LeRoy W.	New York, N.Y.	1843-67
LeRoy W. Fairchild & Co.	New York, N.Y.	1867-73
L. W. Fairchild	New York, N.Y.	1873-86

L. W. Fairchild & Sons	New York, N.Y.	1886–89
LeRoy Fairchild & Co.	New York, N.Y.	1898–1919
Fairchild & Co.	New York, N.Y.	1919–22
Forbes, Abraham Gerritse	New York, N.Y.	1808–30
Forbes, Benjamin G. Fordham & Forbes	New York, N.Y.	1817–39
Forbes, Colin Van Gilder	New York, N.Y.	1808–39
Forbes, C. V. G. & Son		1826–38
Forbes, C. & J. W. Colin and John W.	New York, N.Y.	1810–19
Forbes Garret	New York, N.Y.	1808–30
Forbes, John Wesley J. W. Forbes & Co.	New York, N.Y.	1808–38
Forbes, William Son of C.V.G.	New York, N.Y.	1828–50
Forbes, William Graham	New York, N.Y.	1796–1809
Fueter, Daniel	New York, N.Y.	1786–1806
Fueter, Daniel Christian	New York, N.Y.	1754–76
Fueter, Lewis	New York, N.Y.	1770–74
Gale, William Gale, Wood & Hughes	New York, N.Y.	1824–50
Gale, William & Son	New York, N.Y.	1850–66
Gale, William, Jr. & Co.	New York, N.Y.	1850
Gale, Wood & Hughes William Gale, Jacob Wood	New York, N.Y.	1836–45

and Jasper W. Hughes		
Gale & Hughes	New York, N.Y.	1845–50
William Gale, Jasper W. Hughes		
Gale & Mosely	New York, N.Y.	1828–33
William Gale, Joseph Mosely		
Gale & Stickler	New York, N.Y.	1822–23
William Gale and John Stickler		
Gale & Willis	New York, N.Y.	1840
Galt & Brothers, Inc.	Washington, D.C.	1802
James Galt		
Gardiner, B. & Co.	New York, N.Y.	1835
Gebelein, George C.	Boston, Mass.	1922–71
Gelston, George S.	New York, N.Y.	1833–37
Gelston, Henry	New York, N.Y.	1839
Gelston, Ladd & Co.	New York, N.Y.	1839–43
Gelston & Co.	New York, N.Y.	1836
Gelston & Treadwell	New York, N.Y.	1840
Gleason, R. & Sons	Dorchester, Mass.	1907–46
Gorham, Corp.	Providence, R.I.	1818–present
Jabez Gorham, founder		1818
Gorham & Webster		1831–37
Gorham, Webster & Price		1837–41
Jabez Gorham & Son		1841–50
Gorham & Thurber		1850–52
Gorham & Co.		1852–63
Gorham Manu-facturing Co.		1863–65
Gorham Corpo-ration		1865–present
Greenough, Daniel	New Castle, N.H.	(1655/6–1746)

Harland, Thomas	Norwich, Conn.	(1735?–1807)
Harland, Thomas, Jr.	Norwich, Conn.	(1781–1806)
Hayward, Walter E. Co., Inc.	Attleboro, Mass.	1851–present
Hayward, Thompson & Co.		1851
Charles E. Hayward & Johnathan Briggs, partners		1855
C. E. Hayward & Co.		1855–87
Hayward & Sweet		1887–1904
Walter E. Hayward Co.		1904–08
Frank J. Ryder & Charles Wilmarth purchased		1908
Henchman, Daniel	Boston, Mass.	(1730–75)
Heyer, William B.	New York, N.Y.	1798–1832
Heyer & Nevins		
Heyer & Gale		
Hinsdale, Horace Seymour	New York, N.Y.	1805–58
Taylor & Hinsdale	Newark, N.J. and New York, N.Y.	1807–17
Palmer & Hinsdale	New York, N.Y.	1817–23
Hinsdale & Atkin		1836–38
Thomas G. Brown & Sons		1838–58
Holmes & Edwards Silver Co.	Bridgeport, Conn.	1882–present
George C. Edwards and C. E. L. Holmes		
Part of International Silver Co.		1898
Homan Mfg. Co.	Cincinnati, Ohio	1847–1942
Homan & Co.	Cincinnati, Ohio	1847–1910

Homan Silver Plate Co.	Cincinnati, Ohio	1896–1910
Howard Sterling Co.	Providence, R.I.	1878–1915
H. Howard & Co.		1878–79
Howard & Scherrieble		1879–84
Howard & Son		1884–92
Howard Sterling Co.		1892–present
Hull, John	Boston, Mass.	1624–83
Hurd, Benjamin	Boston and Roxburg, Mass.	1739–81
Hurd, Jacob	Boston, Mass.	(1702/3–58)
Hurd, Nathaniel	Boston, Mass.	(1729/30–77)
International Silver Co.	Meriden, Conn.	1898–present
Jones, Ball & Poor	Boston, Mass.	1846
Jones, Lows & Ball	Boston, Mass.	1839
Kirk, Samuel & Son	Baltimore, Md.	1815–present
Kirk & Smith		1815–20
Samuel Kirk		1821–46
Samuel Kirk & Son		1846–61
Samuel Kirk & Sons		1861–68
Samuel Kirk & Son		1868–96
Samuel Kirk & Son Co.		1896–1924
Samuel Kirk & Son, Inc.		1924–present
Klank, C. & Sons	Baltimore, Md.	1872–1911
Klank & Brother		1872–91
Conrad Klank & Sons		1892–93
C. Klank & Sons Mfg. Co.		1893–94
C. Klank & Sons		1895–1911

Le Roux, Bartholomew	New York, N.Y.	(1663–1713)
Le Roux, Bartholomew II	New York, N.Y.	(1717–63)
Le Roux, Charles	New York, N.Y.	(1689–1745)
Le Roux, John	Albany, N.Y.	1730
Loring, Joseph	Boston, Mass.	(1743–1815)
Lows, John J. Partner Jones, Lows and Ball	Boston, Mass.	(1800–76)
Lowe, Joshua	New York, N.Y.	1828–33
Lunt Silversmiths	Newburyport, Mass.	1883–90
	Greenfield, Mass.	1890–1902
		1935–present
Manchester Silver Co. William H. Manchester	Providence, R.I.	1887–present
W. H. Manchester & Co.		1887–1904
Manchester Mfg. Co.		1904–14
Baker-Manchester Mfg. Co.		1915
Manning, Bowman & Co.	Meriden, Conn.	1850–present
E. B. Manning (Britannia)		1850–75
Manning, Bowman & Co.		1857–1915
Marquand, Frederick	Savannah, Ga.	1820–26
	New York, N.Y.	1826–39
Marquand & Bros.	New York, N.Y.	1814–1831
Marquand & Co. Isaac Marquand and Erastus O. Thompkins	New York, N.Y.	1833–39

Mayo, Benjamin J.	Newark, N.J.	1860–1902
Mead, John O.	Philadelphia, Pa.	1840
Partnership with		
Wm. and Asa		
Rogers	Hartford, Conn.	1845
John O. Mead	Philadelphia, Pa.	1846
Mead & Sons		?
Filley & Mead		?
Filley, Mead &		1850
Caldwell		
Meriden Britannia Co.	Meriden, Conn.	1852–98
Merged into Inter-		1898–present
national Silver Co.		
Moore, Apollos	Albany, N.Y.	1842–50
Moore, Jared	New York, N.Y.	1825–52
	Brooklyn, N.Y.	1843
Moore, J. L. & Co.	New York, N.Y.	1837–44
Jared Moore,		
Charles Brewer,		
Francis Brown		
Moore, John Chandler	New York, N.Y.	1832–44
Moore & Brewer	New York, N.Y.	1840
Jared L. Moore		
Charles Brewer		
Morton, B. R. & Co.	Syracuse, N.Y.	1844–49
Moulton, Abel	Newburyport, Mass.	(1784–?1840)
Moulton, Ebenezor	Boston and Newburyport,	
	Mass.	(1768–1824)
Mulholland Bros.	Aurora, Ill.	1915–22
Murdock, James & Co.	Utica, N.Y.	1826–32
James Murdock,		
Elon Andrews,		
Julius A. Spencer		
Murdock & Andrews	Utica, N.Y.	1822–49
James Murdock and		
Elon Andrews		

Myers, Myer	New York, N.Y.	1753–82
Myers & Halsted	Norwalk, Conn.	1776–80
	Philadelphia, Pa.	1780–82
National Silver Co.	New York, N.Y.	1890–present
Originally Samuel E.		
Bernstein		
Norton & Seymour	Syracuse, N.Y.	1850
B. R. Norton and		
Joseph Seymour		
Onclebagh, Gerrit	New York, N.Y.	1670–1732
Oneida Silversmiths	Sherrill, N.Y.	1877–present
Pairpoint Corpo-	New Bedford, Mass.	1880–1958
ration, The		
Paul Revere Silver	Boston, Mass.	1912–22
Co., Inc.		
Pelletreau, Elias	Southampton, L.I.	1751–76
	Simsbury and Saybrook,	
	Conn.	1782–1810
Pelletreau, Maltby	New York, N.Y.	1815–40
Pelletreau, William	Southampton, L.I.	(1786–1842)
Smith		
Pelletreau &		1810
Van Wyck		
Pelletreau, Bennet	New York, N.Y.	1826–28
& Cooke		
Maltby Pelletreau,		
John Bennett &		
D. C. Cooke		
Pelletreau & Richards	New York, N.Y.	1825
Pelletreau & Upson	New York, N.Y.	1824
Platt, George W.	New York, N.Y.	1824
Platt, G. W. & N. C.	New York, N.Y.	1828–35
Platt, W. A.	New York, N.Y.	1845

Platt & Brother	New York, N.Y.	1835
Platt & Brothers	New York, N.Y.	1836–46
George W.,		
Nathan C., David		
D., Elkana Platt		
Reed & Barton	Taunton, Mass.	1824–present
Babbitt & Crossman		1824
Reed & Barton		1840–present
Revere, Paul	Boston, Mass.	1735–1818
Revere, Paul, Sr.	Boston, Mass.	1702–54
Revere, Thomas	Boston, Mass.	1739–1817
Rice, Joseph T.	Albany, N.Y.	1813–50
Rich, Obadiah	Boston, Mass.	1830–40
Robbins, Charles M.	Attleboro, Mass.	1892–present
Robbins Co.		
Rogers & Britten	West Stratford, Conn.	1880–1904
Rogers & Brother	Waterbury, Conn.	1858–present
Asa Jr. and Simeon		
International Silver		1898–present
Co.		
Rogers Brothers	Waterbury and	1825–present
William Rogers,	Meriden, Conn.	
Joseph Church		
(Church & Rogers)		1825
Rogers & Cole		1830
Asa Rogers Jr. Co.		1832
Rogers Bros. Mfg.		1853
Co.		
William & Asa		1853
Rogers, Jr.		
Rogers, Smith & Co.		1861
International Silver		1898–present
Co.		
Rogers & Hamilton	Waterbury, Conn.	1886–present
Co.		

International Silver Co.		1898–present
Rogers, C. & Brothers Cephas, Gilbert and Wilbur Rogers International Silver	Meriden, Conn.	1866–present
Co.		1903
Rogers, F. B. Silver Co.	Taunton, Mass.	1883–present
Div. National Silver Co.		1955–present
Rogers, Simeon L. & George H. Co. Acq. by Wm. A.	Hartford, Conn.	1900–present
Rogers Ltd. Purchased by		1918
Oneida		1929–present
Rogers, Lunt & Bowlen & Co.	Greenfield, Mass.	1902–present
Roosevelt, Nicholas	New York, N.Y.	1769
Sanderson, Robert	Watertown and Boston, Mass.	1608–93
Sawin, Silas	Boston, Mass.	1823
	New York, N.Y.	1825–28
Sayre, Joel	Southampton, L.I.	1798
	New York, N.Y.	1802–18
Sayre, John	New York, N.Y. Cohoes, N.Y.	1796–1814
Sayre, Paul	Southampton, N.Y.	1785
Sayre & Richards John Sayre and Thomas Richards	New York, N.Y.	1802–18
Seymour, Joseph Mfg. Co.	New York, N.Y. Utica, N.Y.	1835 1842–47
Jos. Seymour, Sons & Co.		1887

Jos. Seymour Mfg. Co.		1909
Shepherd, Robert	Albany, N.Y.	1805–10
Shepherd & Boyd Robert Shepherd and William Boyd	New York, N.Y.	1810–29
Shepherd & Hoyt	Albany, N.Y.	1830
Shiebler, George W. & Co.	New York, N.Y.	1890–1915
Shreve, Crump & Low Co.	Boston, Mass.	1869–present
Simpson, Hall, Miller & Co. Samuel Simpson Part of International Silver Co.	Wallingford, Conn.	1866–present

1898–present |
| Soumaine, Simeon | New York, N.Y. | 1727–44 |
| Stone Associates Arthur Stone | Gardner, Mass. | 1901–55 |
| Taunton Britannia Mfg. Co. Reed & Barton | Taunton, Mass. | 1830–present

1840–present |
| Tiffany & Co. Tiffany & Young Tiffany, Young & Ellis Tiffany & Co. | New York, N.Y. | 1837–present 1837 1841

1853 |
| Towle Silversmiths William Moulton Towle & Jones | Newburyport, Mass. | 1857–present

1857 |
| Tuttle Silversmiths Tuttle Silver Co. Div. of Hamilton Watch Co. | Boston, Mass. | 1890–present 1915 1959 |
| Unger Brothers | Newark, N.J. | 1896–1915 |

Van Bergh Silver Plate Co. Frederick Van Bergh and Maurice H. Van Bergh Oneida Community Ltd.	Rochester, N.Y.	1892–present 1926
Van Voorhis, Daniel	Philadelphia, Pa. Princeton, N.J. New York, N.Y.	1780–82 1782–83 1785, 1797–99
Van Voorhis, Bayley, Coley & Cox	New York, N.Y.	1785
Van Voorhis, Baley & Coley	New York, N.Y.	1784–85
Van Voorhis & Coley Daniel van Voorhis and William Coley	New York, N.Y.	1785–87
Van Voorhis & Schanck Daniel van Voorhis and Gerrit Schanck	New York, N.Y.	1793
Van Voorhis & Son Daniel and Thomas Richard van Voorhis	New York, N.Y.	1798–1805
Wallace Silversmiths Robert Wallace Robert Wallace & Co. Wallace, Simpson & Co. R. Wallace & Sons Mfg. Co. Wallace Silversmiths	Wallingford, Conn.	1834–present 1834 1855 1865 1871 1956

Warner, Thomas H. Andrew Ellicott Warner	Baltimore, Md.	1780–1828
Watson Company	Attleboro, Mass.	1794–present
Cobb, Gould & Co.		1874–94
Watson & Newell		1894–1919
Watson Company		1919–55
Wallace Silversmiths		1955–present
Webster Co. George K. Webster	North Attleboro, Mass.	1869–present
Reed & Barton		1950
Whiting & Davis Co., Inc.	Plainville, Mass.	1876–present
Wallace Co.		1960–present
Whiting Mfg. Co.	Providence, R.I.	1866–present
Gorham Corp.		1905–present
Whiting, Frank M.	North Attleboro, Mass.	1881–present
F. M. Whiting Co.		1881
Frank M. Whiting & Co.		1900
Div. of Ellmore Silver Co.		1940–60
Whitney Jewelry Co.	Boston, Mass.	1883–1911
Whitney Bros.		1883
E. A. Whitney, Company		1894–1911
Wilcox Silver Plate Co.	Meriden, Conn.	1865–present
Jedidiah & Horace Wilcox, Charles Parker, Aaron Collins and Hezekiah Miller		
International Silver Co.		1898–present
Wood, Abraham	Newburgh, N.Y.	1822

Wood, Benjamin Cole & Wood	New York, N.Y.	1806–20
Wood, John	New York, N.Y. Albany, N.Y.	1770
	Schenectady, N.Y.	1780–92
Wood, William S.	Skaneateles, N.Y.	1810–15
Wood & Hughes	New York, N.Y.	1840–99
Young, Otto & Co.	Chicago, Ill.	1865–1924

Bibliography

Avery, Louise C. *Early American Silver*. New York: 1968. Russell & Russell.

Bohan, Peter and Hammerslough, Philip. *Early Connecticut Silver, 1700–1840*, Middletown, Conn.: Wesleyan University Press, 1970.

Buhler, Kathryn C. *American Silver 1655–1825 in the Museum of Fine Arts Boston*. Greenwich, Conn.: New York Graphic Society, 1972.

Buhler, Kathryn C. and Hood, Graham. *American Silver; Garvan and Other Collections in the Yale University Art Gallery*. New Haven, Conn. and London: Yale University Press, 1970.

Ensko, Stephen, G. G. *American Silversmiths and Their Marks*, Vol. III. New York: Robert Ensko, Inc., 1948.

May, Earl Chapin. *A Century of Silver*. New York: Robert M. McBride Co., 1947.

McClinton, Katherine Morrison. *Collecting American 19th Century Silver*. New York: Charles Scribner's Sons, 1968.

Rainwater, Dorothy T. *American Silver Manufacturers*. Hanover, Pennsylvania: Everybodys Press, 1966.

Index